Mission: Leadership

Lifting the Mask

By

BEN MORTON

 mPowr

First published in Great Britain 2017 by
mPowr (Publishing) Limited
www.mpowrpublishing.com

www.theleadershipadvantage.co.uk
www.mpowrpublishing.com

A catalogue record for this book is available from the British Library

ISBN 978-1-907282-71-3

To Mum and Dad,

Thank you for letting go of your son at sixteen..

Thank you for your continual support
and encouragement ever since.

I love you both.

Contents

Section One
War Zone Leadership

Section Two
Covert Leadership

Section Three
Business Leadership

Introduction

After surviving the ever-present threat to life and limb during the Iraq War and the intense pressures of corporate life, I thought that writing this book on leadership would be relatively straightforward...

Leadership is a very serious matter. It is the most critical issue facing business in a complex, volatile and ever-changing world.

I have experienced the leadership of others (at its very best and very worst) in the military and corporate world. I have experienced my own leadership successes as well as moments of disappointment and failure. All of these have formed a strong, powerful vision of leadership that transforms individuals and teams around the world when I work with them as a consultant and mentor.

Many leadership books present a simple model to follow, a *six-steps-to-success* formula. There are some benefits to this approach; however, it does not do leadership justice. Leadership is not a set of behaviours to be imitated or a process to be followed. It is a way of being that empowers, inspires and transforms those around you.

How was I to avoid this simplistic, formulaic approach to leadership so that you can achieve greater results, inspire your team and enjoy the privilege and responsibility of being a great leader?

I thought back to the ways in which I gradually learned, developed and applied the principles of leadership. Whilst leadership is seen most obviously in dramatic situations the foundations are laid in the ordinary, everyday interactions and moments of reflection. It is not what we say or do in the heat of the battle that inspires others to do as we ask. People follow us because of how we connect with them on a day-to-day basis at a truly human level.

I have been a student of leadership from my earliest days, from my parents, my hours immersed in the *Commando* comics and the adventures of my teenage years. The inspiring individuals I've met throughout my own leadership journey and the military ethos of *Serve to Lead* have also played their part.

I chose not to present another dry, serious book on leadership that delivers lots of information but very little transformation. The need for powerful, enlightened leaders is far too urgent for this somewhat familiar approach.

So you are invited to put yourself at the centre of this book—to explore your own experiences, challenges, hopes, fears, strengths, strategies and values. Then you will move ahead with confidence as you develop your own leadership philosophy, based on solid foundations.

Just as I learned the values, skills and strategies of leadership through play, exploration and experimentation, this book is designed to step you through this journey as well.

Alongside my own experiences from the British Army and the corporate world you'll find a series of provocative, playful leadership parables that are designed to help you identify the victims, villains and heroes of leadership—these are not just other people... You will sometimes exhibit the traits of victim, villain or hero... Pay particular attention to the hero. The hero teaches you everything you need long before I get round to explaining it...

Section One ███████████████████

War Zone Leadership

The Adventures of Captain Ben Morton...
The Sniff Test

SOMEWHERE IN
THE KUWAITI DESERT...

SCUD MISSILE,
ONE MILE NORTH...

TIME TO GET MY KIT ON...

Before the last word was shouted, I had instinctively closed my eyes, held my breath and ripped open the pouch on my right hip reaching for my gas mask. With my hands grasping the rubber straps, I thrust my chin into the mask pulling the straps over my head. As I opened my eyes and shouted, "Gas, gas, gas!" myself, I smelt the familiar, stale rubber smell that I had smelled so many times before.

I then looked for the nearest piece of cover and ran a few metres taking shelter underneath the ubiquitous four-tonne army truck. As I hauled myself under that truck with five or six of my soldiers, I checked that everyone was OK. Yet, even though the Gulf War that I was now a part of was very real, I still assumed this was just another false alarm. Until this point there had been no action, and the number of times the gas alert had turned out to be a false alarm had instilled an underlying complacency in me.

My nuclear, biological and chemical (NBC) warfare skills were now such a part of me that I did everything I needed to do without thinking. However, beneath the automatic response of getting my mask on within seven seconds, there remained a knowing that this was just another drill.

This was not just another drill.

Leadership is an alluring and evocative skill. It is often thought that leadership is about controlling others, having some form of power over them, or forcing them to act on one's every command or whim.

I believe that, whilst the effects of leadership can be measured in the actions and behaviours of other people, the foundations of leadership stem from how you serve other people. When you serve to lead, you inspire that same ethos in the hearts and minds of your team. This is at the very core of true leadership.

History is littered with leaders who cajoled others into action by fear and threat, however, the leader who truly inspires their team does not need to rely on forcing people to act against their will. The leader who creates relationships of trust and respect; who is in service of their team—is the one who can galvanise the most profound bond with their people.

When a leader leverages fear to place another person in a position of subservience, they can only ever push that person to the point where the fear is less than the pain they are currently feeling. When a person fears what they are experiencing more than what has been threatened, the control mechanism breaks down and they will resist being told what to do.

When people trust, respect and believe in a leader, not for what they do, but for who they are; those people will march towards their own deaths, knowing that, if the tables were turned, their leader would do the same for them.

Leadership is not what you do... it is who you are.

This was a lesson I learnt in the most palpable and visceral of experiences, one that would affect me to this day.

I was stationed at the centre of the British Army's build-up area in the Kuwaiti desert, just thirty kilometres from the Iraqi border. Less than a mile to the north of the camp a Scud missile had come down and was now spewing a potentially lethal, yellow-green smoke into the air.

A fellow officer from the NBC Cell came to the entrance of the HQ tent and beckoned for me to approach, which I did immediately, still unaware of the real danger that was unfolding just a short walk away from our current location.

As I got to him, he instructed me to take two soldiers towards the fallen missile. We were to conduct the *Two-Man Sniff Test*. And, whilst my response was one of compliance, my head was thrown into a quandary about whether I had heard him correctly. The sniff test... seriously?

The two-man sniff test was a procedure I learnt during my officer training at Sandhurst. In addition to practising the routine for getting into full NBC Kit, we also learnt what to do in various scenarios that involved a nuclear, biological or chemical attack.

The sniff test seemed completely bizarre when I first encountered it. Something so primitive and archaic surely could not be a part of modern warfare?

Two years previously, on a patch of grass in Sandhurst's grounds, a colour sergeant was getting us to role play the sniff test, which is the final procedure for checking that an area is safe before ordering all troops to remove their gas masks. Two soldiers are positioned facing each other, about a metre apart, whilst their commander stands beside them.

The soldiers then take a long, deep breath, filling their lungs. When they have inhaled to capacity they each take two fingers and break the seal on their masks. Lifting the mask away from their faces by just a centimetre, they take a tiny sniff of air. Now, because their lungs are already full, this last bit of breath would be minuscule, but if the air were contaminated, it would still have an effect on them.

Once the last sniff of air was taken all three would watch for signs of contamination by a nerve agent or poison. From the pin-pricking of pupils to body tremors, and so on, staring at a fellow soldier who could be dying beneath the dark black fascia of the mask was somewhat surreal.

I took turns to perform this, both in the part of the soldier and the officer. It was a very simple routine, but so strange in that simplicity, because it was two soldiers risking their lives for the sake of others. Such a grave sacrifice masquerading as the simple lifting of a mask; it seemed utterly removed from anything I would actually be asked to do in my army career.

However, here I was, being ordered to carry out that very same test in an extremely real, life-threatening war. So, now I had to make my way back to the four-tonne truck where I had been sheltering moments before and order two men to risk their lives on my say-so.

Part of my Sandhurst training was that of a solider; foundation training that encompassed the basics, such as... how to survive on a battlefield. I was also taught how to lead others into conflict; an essential aspect of being an officer.

Leadership was presented, not as a list of processes or a set of steps that we did, but the person we became. I discovered that being a leader was more about the perspective you experience the world from, rather than a model you try to fit the world into.

The power of what I learnt at Sandhurst was that a leader did not demonstrate their leadership by giving commands—they proved their leadership through a myriad of factors that took place long before a single command was ever given.

By the time that moment came when I asked those two soldiers to risk their lives, I was already assured of their unquestioning loyalty. Some may say that, as soldiers, these two men were trained to obey orders; that as mere squaddies, they would just obey regardless of the context, all because of my rank.

I believe the reason they sprang into action willingly and without hesitation was precisely the opposite—it was because I related to them as people, rather than expendable things.

I knew both of those men as individuals with complex and multifaceted lives; they each had a mother at home who was worried senseless, as was mine. They had fathers and brothers and sisters; they had girlfriends; they were loved. And if they died on that day, in that place, their loss would be grieved by countless other people. The pain would not be over, for it would impact the daily lives of their loved ones for a lifetime.

The two soldiers and I walked across the sand in silence, away from the safety of the camp and towards our fate. As we took each step forward, I found myself checking that I was prepared for what came next; from the procedure if there were some noxious agent in the air, to the combi-pen set I carried in my kit— three EpiPen-like devices that, when injected, would each buy a soldier twenty minutes of life enabling them, hopefully, to reach a field hospital.

The consequences of these fleeting moments affected all three of us; however, I would only know to what extent many months later. Whilst they would be the ones taking the risk of breathing toxic gas, I was with them every step of the way, valuing their lives as I would my own.

This is leadership. This is what it means to be a leader.

In this book, we shall explore what it truly means to be a leader, and how you can evolve into your own unique perspective of leadership. As we explore the principles of leadership and what it means to be a leader, I will guide you step by step though the secrets that I have uncovered not only in my career as an officer in the British Army, but also as an operative in a very different context; the corporate world of business.

Your mission, should you choose to accept it, is to strip away the myths, misinterpretations and dogma of leadership, to develop a new way of being the best you can be, professionally, personally and as part of a team.

There are many dynamic and effective insights to share with you, and whilst these are both rich and diverse in nature, they can be summed up in effect by that one moment of time. That moment when I watched those two men, standing beside me. Two men who came to the end of their breath, and without a pause for doubt or misgiving, raised their hands and lifted their masks to take one last sniff...

THE TWO-MAN SNIFF TEST

Mission One: The Sniff Test

Your first mission:

To infiltrate and navigate the terrain of your leadership experiences and return with intelligence on your skills as a leader.

Retrieve the following information, make notes about and record any other discoveries you feel are relevant.

Whilst the consequences of what you ask your people to do may not be so great, you will need to make big requests of your people from time to time. Do those that you have the privilege to lead, trust, respect and believe in you enough to lift their masks for you?

How far will your team go for you?

Do you view your role as one of management or of leadership?

Mission One Checklist

Before reading any further in this book, it is important to understand what it truly means to be a leader. We must also remember the extraordinary things that people are prepared to do when they trust and believe in their leader.

The most effective leaders are those that create strong relationships with their teams based upon trust and respect.

When people trust, respect and believe in a leader, not for what they do, but for who they are; they will march towards their own deaths knowing that, if the tables were turned, their leader would do the same for them.

Leadership is not what you do... it is who you are.

LATEST NEWS...
INCREASING TENSIONS IN THE MIDDLE EAST
PROVOKE FEARS OF ANOTHER GULF WAR...

The Nature of Leadership... Unsolved

...AS THE ARMY PREPARE FOR DEPLOYMENT, THE SOLDIERS READY THEMSELVES FOR WAR.

During the Iran-Iraq war, Iraq used chemical weapons on its own people and early in 2003 the rumours of possible Iraqi chemical and biological capability were ever-prominent in the news. The British media were reporting on the increasing tensions in the Middle East and how a second Gulf War was now imminent.

We were preparing for deployment to Kuwait with the issuing of kit, receiving a series of anthrax jabs and then, once the campaign began, we were ordered to start taking Nerve-Agent-Pretreatment-Set (NAPS) tablets. Between the media frenzy and the historical actions of Iraq, I became increasingly aware of what was about to happen... and it felt very real.

If the Iraqis could kill their own people what potential horrors were they prepared to do to us? Where would they draw a line between fear of what they were doing (and the consequences if they did not do it) and fear of how the allies would act in retaliation?

The simple lifting of a mask under a threat so real, so utterly deadly, is not something we can assume is simple. To truly appreciate what those two men were sacrificing by removing their masks, we need to look deeper into what they, you, and I have to give. Furthermore, to understand the level of trust and respect required to give that thing, we also need to explore what it means to be a leader.

Attempting to grasp the real nature of leadership in a definitive way can be compared to the pursuit of holding on to sand or water. The harder you try to clench it in your hand—to control it or assert authority over it—the faster it trickles away from you.

A true understanding of leadership comes with an appreciation for the underlying principles of leaders, rather than the outward effects of their actions. I could list off how I would choose to act in various scenarios, but these would be symptoms of leadership, and would not present you with a real insight into what those decisions are based upon.

To know the reasons behind leadership choices, we need to go further back to explore the building blocks of leadership that I encountered long before being a leader. Those very first steps into achieving my own leadership advantage came in childhood, before I was even aware of who I was to become as an adult.

At first glance, I was not born into any substantial leadership traditions. The extent of that particular aspect of my heritage came from both my grandads. My mum's dad, Reg, spent his wartime in the Merchant Navy. He would speak a little about his experiences when I asked questions, especially when I was doing a school project on WWII.

At the age of twelve, I watched, with my family, a news report on the First Gulf War. I was fascinated by the footage of soldiers practising in the desert. There was a moment the soldiers donned their gas masks and shouted, "Gas, gas, gas!" and my grandad replied, almost by reflex, "Gas, gas, gas!"

My dad's father, Hugh, served as a sergeant in the Royal Military Police at the end of World War II, but he never spoke about his experiences. This was the extent of my immediate family's connection to the military.

However, my parents instilled within me the values and foundations of leadership—for being a parent is the most fundamental leadership position of all. Therefore, even though my mum and dad were not leaders in any formal, or recognised way, their own leadership principles nurtured within me my aspirations for being a leader.

Of all the foundations they gave me, there are three that stand out beyond all others:

- Work hard for what you want and invest your time.

- Do what you believe to be the right thing, rather than the easy thing.

- Put the needs of others first—ahead of your own needs if necessary.

My dad taught me the importance of working for what you want. The value in achieving rewards by striving for them, as opposed to relying on credit, has stayed with me. He held down several jobs, from delivering mushrooms for market, to his portering at Spitalfields in London. He would leave home at three each morning to arrive before the market opened.

Occasionally he would take me into work for the day. I would nestle on his lap as he drove the forklift truck and milk float, which carried the fruit and vegetables around the market. The memories of those times bring a smile, even if it is a poignant one.

My parents stayed together through the breakdown of their marriage, and they did it for my sister and I. Choosing to do the right thing for the sake of their children could not have been easy, but they committed to that path anyway.

Now, I am not advocating staying in relationships that are irrevocably broken... I remember the arguments and how painful they were. As a parent now I would not do the same, but absolutely understand why they did it and admire the values behind it. I can appreciate how difficult it must have been for them, because every one of those rows demonstrates just how committed they were to us, and the depth of their own sacrifice for the sake of our well-being.

Putting the needs of others first did not stop there; my mum did not want me to join the Army. Yet, she supported me all the way, because she knew how much I wanted it.

As she watched me walking down the long driveway of Welbeck, the army sixth-form college, she wept. Although I was sixteen at the time, she was saying goodbye to her precious baby boy and it was absolutely heartbreaking for her. My dad looked at her and, in his own inimitable way, said, "Imagine how you'd feel if he hadn't got in!"

This is the foundation of real leadership, when watching somebody leave it is tough, but witnessing their dreams being shattered is tougher. No matter how challenging it was for her she knew it was the right thing for me.

This was the end of a very long road for both me and my parents. It was a journey that had begun when I was eight years old and mum and dad had taken me to the summer fete at Brentwood Sports Centre. As we wandered amongst the different stalls, one particular stand took my attention—*Army Recruiting*.

I stood mesmerised, by the various posters and weapons on display, to the extent that my mother noticed this was no cursory glance. It was at that moment she knew I was destined to join the army, and it filled her with dread. Although, rather than giving in to her concerns, she decided that, if I was indeed going to enlist, I would do so as an officer.

Of course, this stemmed from the notion that army officers are somehow nice and safe, out of harm's way. No matter how misguided this belief is, it instilled within me a career goal that is hardly ever seen in business. It set my heart and my focus on becoming a leader by trade.

In most career paths that people venture upon, they want to do something; from driving trains to joining a pop group, it is about doing the job. In some cases, the specific role boils down to the basics of earning money... a career is something that pays the bills and nothing more. Very few people enter into the business world to be a leader; it is a way to progress, increase salary, and nothing more.

Regardless of my mum's thoughts on my career in the army, I did not decide until much later that this was what I wanted to do. My next constructive steps to becoming a leader in the forces came at fourteen, when I joined the Army Cadets. At this point in my life, I had made a definite decision on the career I wanted; it was time to start honing my skills as a leader...

In my book *Don't Just Manage—Coach!,* I list three components of a leader's role, which are:

- Doing things
- Managing Things
- Leading People

Becoming an army cadet was me doing things. Learning how to actually do the job, firstly through the cadet training, but also outside of this setting as I invested time in studying and role-playing. Gradually I became obsessed and would voraciously read anything and everything I could on the army and leadership.

Even that early in my military career there were the initial signs of managing things and leading people.

At fourteen I had not created a formal strategy around managing my goals, as I would now. Then, it was driven by raw obsession and desire. I threw myself into learning, because I loved it so much and desperately wanted it.

Most of us can recall at least one anecdote of how our parents caught us in a compromising position, and I am no exception. Though when my father caught me, it was when he walked in on me practising the NBC warfare drill!

My father was not the only one to unexpectedly witness the results of my passion for all things military. After watching a video of the 1988 SAS siege of the Iranian Embassy, I came to the conclusion that I utterly needed to abseil out of my bedroom window. So, I tied a rope around the radiator and tossed the other end from the first-floor window.

I was in position in the open window, preparing to rappel down the wall, when my mum walked in and put a stop to my impromptu covert ops. As if this was not enough for my poor mother, I also enjoyed creating traps to catch animals in the woodland at the bottom of our garden.

Of course, once a trap had been expertly rigged what better way to test the trap than on one's own mother? I would ask her to come and stand at a particular spot in the woods, which she would do despite being terrified that an enormous log was about to swing down from the branches of a nearby tree and finish her off!

When I wasn't terrorising my parents, I would read anything I could get my hands on that involved the army. From books on British Army tactics to the *Commando* comics, I would devour everything that might improve my military and leadership skills in some way.

It was from this I learnt how extremely valuable these books are—so be proud of your books on leadership. Never hide them away or treat them as a weakness; instead leave them on display or share them with your team.

These essential learning tools are a sign of your strength and determination as a leader. Showing that you are continually working on your own skill set is a demonstration of authenticity in your leadership—that you are as prepared and willing as your team to do what is necessary to achieve greatness.

Mission Two: The Nature of Leadership... Unsolved

This mission consists of two specific tasks.

Task One: to understand the type of leader you want to be.

Many people in business do not want to be a leader! Your mission here is to solve the nature of leadership and develop an in-depth understanding of what leadership means for you... and how you will master your craft.

Solving the mysteries of true leadership is not about your background or ancestry. It requires commitment to studying and mastering the craft of leadership. A master in any field will strive for over ten thousand hours in passionate research and practice to achieve their goal. They literally eat, sleep and breathe what they want to do.

To become a leader, you need to want it and understand what that means.

To begin with you need to understand what you stand for. You must first get really clear on your values so that you are able to use these as the foundations for how you operate as a leader.

Our values are the things that are most important to us as we live our lives at work and at home. They are the underlying beliefs that drive our actions on a conscious and unconscious basis. Our values are generally non-physical constructs such as honesty, freedom or connection.

Look at the values cloud and highlight or underline any that really resonate with you. Add your own personal values. Then take time to reflect on the values that really stand out for you and why. Create a list of the most important values, five or six, that provide the foundations for your personal leadership.

Honesty

Integrity Freedom

Connection

Fairness Growth Challenge

Collaboration Family

Autonomy

Balance Adventure

Happiness

Task Two: to understand where you are investing your time right now—are you doing, managing or leading?

This task involves further reconnaissance work. First of all, look at your diary and take a typical day from the last week.

Next, for every activity consider whether you were doing things, managing things or leading people.

If the list appears unbalanced, especially if you are investing little time in leading people, then identify three things that you could either:

- Start doing,
- Stop doing,
- Or delegate to a team member

... allowing you to lead more.

Mission Two Checklist

It is easy for us to look at great leaders in public life or from history and assume that they were natural, gifted leaders. When looking at these individuals we often only see their actions, we do not see their backstory. We do not see the leadership journey that led them to their success.

- Strong leadership is built upon trust and respect between the leader and their team.
- Great leaders put the needs of others ahead of their own.
- Becoming an effective leader takes time and commitment. In fact, our leadership journey never ends and the most dangerous time is the time when we think we have nothing left to learn.
- Great leaders have an insatiable appetite for learning, growth and continual improvement.

Assemble Your Team

It was a day after the start of the second Gulf War when I found myself staring at BBC News 24 in a Kuwaiti port. Images of British and US Marines fighting in the port of Umm Qasr flashed in front of me as I sat, feeling quietly numb.

The day before, my regiment had moved north from the British Army's staging area in the desert of northern Kuwait. We had positioned ourselves some twenty kilometres south of the Iraqi border, where we camouflaged the vehicles and dug a series of shell scrapes. These makeshift trenches were used to protect us from Scud missile attacks.

During the night, there had been frequent shouts of "incoming" from the OC, or officer commanding, which sparked a frenzied sprinting to the trenches. The warnings were coming from the Royal Artillery's early warning system, which tracked missiles in the air nearby. As we took cover, we knew that somewhere, out there in darkness, potential death was closing in.

We had travelled from the normality of our daily lives, to this place so very far from home, and were now huddled in trenches that we had dug for ourselves... we did not know from one moment to the next if these holes would be our graves. There is nothing quite like the imminent threat of missile strikes to wake one up to the realisation of where you are and what you are doing.

Sleep did not come easy that night. I would descend into the briefest moments of troubled slumber, before waking sharply at the realisation of my strange surroundings and the ever-present threat of danger.

I can remember waking at one point and feeling droplets of liquid on my face; the only part of me that was not cocooned in my sleeping and bivvy bags. The smell of acrid smoke, flames and fuel filled my senses, causing my eyes to snap open. The sky was black with smoke, and there was an ominous glow of fire to the north.

My initial reaction to those tiny drops was one of fear and panic. I was enveloped in smoke, and all I could surmise was there had been a chemical attack. In the next few moments, time seemed to slow down and seconds seemed like an eternity.

Then my logical brain kicked in and I realised it was raining. As the war had now begun, the smoke was probably from the burning oil fields to the north; a repeat of what had occurred in 1991. Able to rationalise the situation, I settled back and tried to sleep again, my body and mind wracked with a sickening afterglow of shock and adrenalin.

The following morning I was called to Squadron HQ to an Orders Group, where I was given an overview of my orders. My troop would be attached to the Port and Maritime Regiment. Our mission was to secure a key, strategic objective... the only port in Iraq, Umm Qasr.

As part of the commanding officer's reconnaissance party the first step of my mission was to brief my soldiers for action—I could formulate a more detailed and complex strategy later, but for now I needed to maximise the little time we had.

After briefing my soldiers with what is known as a *warning order*, I would be going ahead to gather further intelligence. This would give me a moment's pause to develop my plan by the time my own troop joined me there. This process of concurrent activity is one of the British Army's Principles of War. Here, the warning order consists of a brief overview that enabled my troop to begin their preparations, whilst I attained full details of the mission and formulated a detailed strategy.

I had completed a year of training at Sandhurst. I had read *Combat and Survival* magazine since the age of thirteen. I had completed the Platoon Commanders Battle Course for Infantry Officers, but nothing had prepared me to manage the security of a huge port. The importance of this key, strategic asset to the coalition was enormous in a way that I could not get my head around, and with no real world experience at all, I was initially unsure of even where to begin.

It was then I remembered a single piece of wisdom that has stayed with me through my life, both in the military and beyond. In *Don't Just Manage—Coach!* I recalled the words of a major from the army recruitment team speaking to me in my school careers office. He told me to "Remember that as a leader, you do not need to have all of the answers."

Being a leader is not about knowing everything, it is about appreciating how you tap into the experience of those who know how to overcome the challenge at hand. Many assume that a leader needs to know everything so they can tell people what to do. A true leader does not need to know everything; they only need to know who in their team to go to in each situation they encounter.

In this situation I decided to take my most experienced corporal with me. Nobody suggested I take him. There was no obligation, no definitive right or wrong thing to do—it just seemed that I could take better responsibility for my troop and my mission with him by my side. Corporal Joe Rushbrook had at least ten years experience in the Army, compared to my eighteen months out of Sandhurst.

To have the advantage of tapping directly into this degree of experience seemed the most natural course of action. Anything else would be stemming from arrogance, rather than leadership. A true leader never allows being a *leader* to get in the way of *being* a leader.

Just in that single act, I demonstrated to my soldiers that I recognised their expertise and experience. I very clearly stated through my choice, not only that I was a competent leader, but more importantly that I trusted them.

Trust is crucial between a leader and their team. It is always reciprocal and cannot be instilled through commanding another person to offer their trust. It is only when you trust them they will trust you. Consider Ernest Hemingway's words...

"The best way to find out if you can trust somebody is to trust them."

According to the research of Jim Kouzes and Barry Posner, authors of *The Leadership Challenge*, there are four desirable qualities that people seek in a trusted leader. These are honesty, vision, inspiration and competence. The more you demonstrate these traits to your team, the more they will trust your ability.

By asking Corporal Rushbrook to accompany me, I was showing my competence as leader, being honest about my need for having the finest support available when making life-or-death decisions, demonstrating my forward-thinking vision for the best chances of success in our mission, and inspiring others through my action.

At the time, I had no knowledge of this research or the factual basis behind it. I simply chose what I believed to be the best course of action. This ability for me grew out of a fundamental joy in the team. Throughout my life I always took great pride in a sense of identity that was more than just me.

As a kid at primary school, I would usually be forming and running a club of some kind and getting friends to join. I would create folders for every member, along with a badge, membership cards, and so on. The feeling of being connected to other people and of working together for some greater achievement was integral to my identity. My love for the team was so profound that in Army Cadets I wanted to create permanent teams, akin to army sections.

These teams would train, develop skills and become accustomed to working together in a very powerful way. This was not something suggested by the adult instructors, it was devised and driven by me for no other reason than I loved being part of a high-performing team. Without any pre-existing teams, I simply took the lead to create them, more from a desire to be a part of them than any notion of leadership.

I even involved my mum, who—having recovered from the random onslaught of siege and entrapment—helped me to make insignia flashes to go on our jackets. This pride in the badge is something I have kept with me to this day. It is not about some great insight or complex intellectual pursuit—it's not rocket science—it is about time and commitment.

Building and nurturing relationships is at the heart of teams and leadership. Just as the difference between two people dating and a marriage is the degree of time and commitment each requires, any relationship needs a consistent investment of these two ingredients to evolve into something meaningful and strong.

In the same way I nurtured those clubs and teams in my younger days, the connection that had grown between my soldiers and I was not achieved in a single act or choice. It took time and commitment. There were many choices I made before that day which encouraged trust, respect, and loyalty. There would be many others after that day. The choice to recognise Corporal Rushbrook's skills and experience was simply one of many that a leader makes every day.

It was on 21st March, 2003, when the Second Gulf War began and, after months of preparation, it only took a day to be thrown into the midst of feeling totally unprepared for what happened next. Heading south with my driver/radio operator and Corporal Rushbrook, I was facing a situation unlike anything I had encountered before. The only way I would be able to do the best I could, was to rely on those around me; my team. Our success was intrinsically linked, and I needed to trust them, in the same way as I would believe in myself to come through for the leaders I trusted and respected.

And now I sat, watching the footage of a war zone—a war zone in southern Iraq where, in less than a day, I would be finding myself and around thirty of my soldiers. I reflected on the previous night's disturbances and wondered if in a few short hours we would be facing a much more real and deadly threat. Then my thoughts turned to what we were going to do about it...

Mission Three: Assemble Your Team

This mission consists of three tasks.

Task One: To ensure your team has a sense of Esprit de Corps.

Are the relationships within your team big, strong and close enough to enable you to become a true high performing team? When teams feel connected and have a sense of belonging, their performance improves dramatically.

What can you do to create a sense of team identity, pride in the badge or Esprit de Corps? On a behavioural level it could involve:

- Developing a Team Charter—behavioural guidelines for how you work together.
- Eating lunch together once a week
- Team social events

On a more practical level it may include:

- A team shirt or uniform for specific events
- A team brand or logo for name cards, notice boards, presentations, etc.

Task Two: To play to your strengths.

Not having to have all of the answers applies equally to those in your team as it does to you as a leader. Does everyone in your team fully understand the strengths, expertise and experience of every team member?

If the answer is no, then you need to allocate specific time to exploring this as a team. When teams are truly clear on each other's strengths and know who to ask for support, what they achieve far exceeds the sum of their individual skills.

Task Three: To apply the Principles of War.

Many leaders do not communicate enough information, and they do not communicate early enough. The incorrect and outdated assumption that leaders need to have all of the answers leads us to withhold information from our teams until we have formulated our own plan. This misguided belief slows down the speed at which our teams and organisations work and often allows our more agile competitors to get ahead of us.

Your task is to begin using the *warning order* concept to allow concurrent activity to take place. Look for every opportunity to brief your team early. Share what information you have and be clear about what you do or do not want them to do next.

Mission Three Checklist

In order to lead a great team you must focus on the team. And whilst you may be the leader that doesn't mean that you have to be the smartest person in the room or even have all of the answers.

- Great leaders deliver results by enlisting the support and skills of those around them.
- Letting go of the need and desire to have all of the answers allows leaders to truly unlock the potential of their team.
- Trust is the critical element that holds teams together and allows them to achieve incredible things.
- Asking for help does not erode your credibility as a leader. It deepens trust and strengthens your position as a leader.
- Communicating early in a high trust environment allows concurrent activity to flourish, speeding up the rate at which you deliver results.

Know Your Team

21ST MARCH, 2003...

...THE SECOND GULF WAR BEGINS!

ALLIED FORCES BATTLE TO SECURE THE PORT OF UMM QASR...

The battle of Umm Qasr had been brutal. Initial predictions of fairly light resistance had underestimated the level of gunfire and mortar attacks, the first troop of US Marines encountered. Soldiers made a tactical withdrawal toward the Kuwaiti border as artillery exploded overhead. Unexpected and at times chaotic, it took a regroup and advancement with tanks before many Iraqis surrendered.

Shortly after the coalition forces moved into the port of Umm Qasr, the remaining Iraqi soldiers either withdrew north to Basra or removed their uniforms and replaced them with civilian clothes. This brief lull in the major fighting was to be a temporary thing, and throughout my time in the port, the tensions remained high—as did the evolving threat of guerrilla warfare.

We never spoke about our fear, but we felt it. The thought of leaving the safety of the compound and going into an environment of alien sights and smells would cause the heart to race and throat to tighten. Everybody we encountered was treated with a degree of mistrust; we questioned their motives and underlying intentions—were they friend or foe? Were they watching our patterns and attempting to decipher how we were operating? Were the actions of seemingly good intent actually meant to thwart us?

All the while we patrolled in soft hats (rather than helmets), so that we appeared non-threatening in the hearts and minds of the civilians. This well-known British tactic helped us to present a less-threatening persona, but did nothing for our own feelings of safety.

On one patrol, we left the compound and stepped off the road, heading across a wide area of sandy wasteland. We were simply doing what we had done several times before, but on this occasion a young boy ran up to me and explained, through an interpreter, that we were about to walk through a minefield. We had no way of knowing if this was true, or merely a deception to stop us from heading further along that path. Either way, we retraced our steps, hurriedly!

Of course, over time these adrenalin-fuelled patrols turned into complacency—a state that is the enemy of any leader. As we became more comfortable leaving the compound, I needed to ensure I guarded against treating each patrol with anything less than a focused and responsive attitude.

Complacency was not really an issue at the port of Umm Qasr, which was an impossible task. The perimeter of the port was around two kilometres, with a stretch of around half a kilometre that faced out to open ocean. Every few hundred metres along the high concrete wall was a lookout tower, although with only thirty people in my team, it was impossible to secure the perimeter effectively.

All we could do was man the main gate and a couple of the towers, with a roving patrol (Quick Reaction Force) in a Land Rover, who would respond to incidents. In the event of serious attacks, we would struggle to maintain our position.

And so it was, with a mission that required more manpower than was actually available, we settled in to defend the borders of this key asset. We were often reminded of how few we were and how many lay beyond that wall.

The locals would gather at night and smash holes in the wall. Often we would get to their location in time to stop them from doing too much damage, however there were a few occasions when they succeeded in breaking completely through the wall.

To plug these newly-made excavations, we would position huge shipping containers in front of the holes, only for a new void to appear in another part of the perimeter. This soon began to resemble a giant game of *Whack Attack*, as we waited for new breaches to conceal with cargo containers, like a child would grasp their giant hammer in readiness for a creature to pop out of their multicoloured burrow!

A few nights into our time at Umm Qasr my quick reaction force received reports of suspected enemy activity taking place in a compound overlooking the port. It was late and there was little time to formulate a detailed plan, so I had to think on my feet—literally!

As soon as I was told about the sightings, I ran to my troop, developing a strategy as I ran. There are times in leadership when we hand control over to the team (or to specific members of the team), trusting them to do their best for the team overall... then, there are moments when we need to take charge and command our teams; this was one of those occasions.

I briefed my troop on the plan, still formatting the final touches as I spoke. My troop sergeant would take a soldier to high ground where they would have a better vantage point over the port. They would carry with them the heavy machine gun and mortar. If they heard gunfire, their orders were to fire parachute flares into the sky.

I took the quick reaction force in the Land Rover to just outside the compound where the activity had been seen. Leaving a few men with the vehicle to provide covering fire should we need it, I went first, guiding the rest of the team along the sandbanks toward the compound.

Remaining undercover, we crawled through some barbed wire to a position that allowed us to watch through our night-sights. Our hearts were racing, and I focused on what I had to do rather than focus on the pounding in my chest, it was time for strong leadership and I could not falter now.

With no immediate sign of activity, we shuffled along the ground, further into the compound and whatever awaited us there. At times such as this, I did not think about my own mortality; my military training just kicked in and enabled me to focus purely on the mission. I only thought of what I needed to do; what the army refer to as drills. These are the elements one is taught and practise about patrolling, handling your kit and weapon, and so on.

With so much on our minds, I suspect that commanders in the military often find this easier than private soldiers. The team, the mission, the radio, timings, where everybody is, the environment, running through various scenarios and the reactions to them—all these aspects provide an excellent distraction to dwelling on one's own fate.

Private soldiers think about the person to their left and their right... that is all they need to think about, meaning their minds are freer to wonder how this might all end. Appreciating this possibility—of my troop thinking about their own mortality—is something I regret not paying more attention to as a young leader. Now I would be more aware of the potential experiences that my team may encounter, when I am busy entrenched in the endeavours of leadership.

Yet, for any naiveté I possessed during my time as a military leader, there is one thing that I knew above all else... the people I was responsible for, were all sons and daughters. Realising that you are responsible for the lives of others and that those people have family, who care deeply about them, brings our responsibility as leaders into sharp focus; regardless of whether we lead on the battlefield or in the boardroom.

They have parents, just as you and I have—for most there is no greater bond between two people than that between a parent and child. In the face of that love, we as leaders, take on that same duty of care when a mother entrusts us with the safety and well-being of their child.

My second posting in the army was to an army training regiment (ATR) in Bassingbourn. This junior entry ATR took sixteen-year-old kids, at the youngest age they could be to join the army, and guided them through a twenty-week course. This was much longer than the usual twelve weeks and was, for nearly all, the longest they had been parted from their mothers.

I was a captain at the time and second-in-command for the training company of around twenty instructors and one-hundred-and-twenty new-found recruits. The first day of a new intake would be the most profound; these nervous boys and girls would arrive with parents who were even more worried than their children.

I viewed my role in this situation as one of talking with the parents and reassuring them. I would look into the terrified eyes and remember my own mum, when she had watched me walk away, seven years prior.

This was not merely a case of bedside manner, with platitudes and lip-service to the degree of responsibility I was taking on. A mother knows when the person they are trusting with their most precious of all things is being authentic. In that moment, I was the person who represented an organisation that could potentially be leading their baby into conflict and mortal danger. They absolutely needed to know I was genuine in my assurances of care and that we would do all we could to bring their child home safely.

To care about your team is an essential aspect of leadership... and you cannot fake it. The care you bring to your role and your team must be real. In business, we may not routinely lead our team into life-or-death situations, but we are still leading daughters, sons, mothers, fathers, wives, husbands, brothers, sisters, grandparents, and people who are loved. We spend 19% of our lives at work, and 35% of our waking time is invested in the workplace.

Everybody should be able to go to work and feel inspired, supported, happy, valued, and cared-for. Ensuring this is how your team feels is your responsibility as their leader. And, whilst the context may be different, the responsibility is exactly the same... These essential elements of the workplace are derived from great leadership and denied to us because of poor leadership.

Caring for your team in a genuine and heartfelt way stems from knowing your team... and you get to know your team by investing time with them individually. In Iraq and Kuwait, I would visit the watchtowers and simply be with my soldiers. Such as the time I stood on the platform of a giant, port-side crane in Kuwait with a young Fijian soldier. He was preparing for his driving test when we returned to the UK and I tested him on *The Highway Code* as we stood guard over the flow of British Army equipment flooding into Kuwait.

This practice of really getting to know my team, by spending time with them, was second nature to me, as I had developed the habit of taking a real interest in my team. On training exercises in the Brecon Beacons, I would leave the warmth and comfort of my sleeping bag and venture out into the cold, wet night to chat to my soldiers. Here I would take the time to get to know them whilst they were on sentry duty, or stag as it is more commonly known; and I did this on their terms, doing what they did, in the environment they were in.

The Welsh call their country *God's Country*—on those cold, dark and wet nights it felt less like God's Country and more like a godforsaken country! Regardless, I would crawl into the stag position—a shallow hole dug into the ground where two soldiers could only just lie, side by side. Here the rain would be invariably drumming on the thin camouflage sheet strung onto trees above to keep the worst of the rain off. In the early hours of the morning, I would have a whispered chat with the soldiers; get to know them and show I cared... they were not just numbers.

Knowing your team has to come from an authentic place; from knowing what it is to be a leader and why you are a leader. You cannot simply apply a model to this process, or truly achieve it because you have an obligation to do so.

Getting to know your team is a very human thing. When you care about your team as individuals, you create a genuine connection and degree of trust that does not come from position alone. Just being a leader, does not entitle you to a team's respect and compliance without question. True leadership is an emotional, value-driven thing. It is fragile and can be broken easily, yet it is also so strong, it can lead people into war zones without hesitation.

If I was going to take soldiers to war and ask them to put their lives at risk, which they did, then they needed to know that I knew them. They needed to know that I cared about them, loved them, and was doing everything I could to keep them safe, because they were real people with lives and families. They would follow me and believe in me.

At Sandhurst, I was taught to keep a troop bible, in which I would record details about my troop. This was far more than my makeshift version of a personal HR file... it was created by interviewing each soldier and gleaning a clear understanding of who they were.

The troop bible contained all the personal details about my soldiers, for instance, name, date of birth, army number, and so on. I would also use the little notebook to jot down memories about my soldier's interests, their family, wives, partners, girlfriends, home town, football team and other fascinating morsels from their lives.

It is very important to remember that caring for your team does not mean you are their best friend or need to socialise with them. This means there is a line to be drawn between being the professional leader and knowing your people. For example, if you socialise with your team, a time will arrive for you to say your farewells and head home before they do.

This sense of distance is something that I once misjudged in a rather bad way... the results of my mistake caused me a lot of trouble and undermined my abilities as a leader.

I had been tasked with heading to a firing range in South Wales, where we were engaged in a series of construction duties. These included, rebuilding ranges, constructing pop-up targets and a series of firing points for soldiers to fire from walls, windows, piles of rubble, and so on. It was summertime and the heat made the work brutally hard, especially in the midday sun!

That evening my troop headed into town for some beers after a very long day; as a second lieutenant, I accompanied them to a local pub. At around ten-thirty, all was well when my troop sergeant came to me and said, "Boss, I'm heading home—are you coming?".

My reply and my subsequent actions would come back to bite me, "No, I'm going to stay for another one with the lads."

Shortly after his departure, a brawl involving my troop broke out in the bar, and I found myself breaking it up. As I strode into the thick of it, I remembered another talk at Sandhurst about there being a time to come and a time to go. The very clear advice I recalled from my platoon commander was, when your platoon sergeant leaves you leave too!

Once the bar brawl had finished, local constabulary arrived upon the scene. After a brief chat with them, my soldiers quickly left. Wanting to do the right thing (rather than the easy thing), I spoke to the landlord and promised him that we, the British Army, would sort it all out.

The following Monday I found myself in front of my commanding officer as he read a line from a letter he had received from the pub landlord describing the incident as "...like a scene from the OK Corral!" (this was an exaggeration in my mind—although I did watch the film to be sure). The landlord also mentioned how Lieutenant Morton had promised that the army would pay for the damage.

Despite the fact the bar brawl should never have happened at all, as an officer I certainly should not have been in the thick of it. There is a time to come and a time to go. As leaders we are always leaders, whether we are on- or off-duty, whether we are in work, at a work social function or out of work—we are still leaders.

Looking back, I now understand there to be two fundamental aspects of my role as a leader in the military.

1. To carry out the orders I was given by my superiors.
2. To look after the soldiers in my command.

There were times these two duties would be in conflict and I would have to make tough decisions, take a stand according to my values and even take calculated risks—yet they remained my priorities regardless.

Keeping the port of Umm Qasr secure, whilst looking after my troop with few resources and not enough manpower was challenging. I requested additional support from my own regiment—however, there was very little that could be done. Major Tim Muir personally came to the port and told me there were no further troops to offer me and that we must make do.

This meant we would regularly move soldiers between the watchtowers, making it look as though we had a bigger force than we did. Sometimes leaders need to think creatively, especially when the job at hand is not a pleasant one and there are not enough resources to deal with it effectively; be these people, equipment, or time, etc.

It was after leading the quick reaction force out to the other compound, which thankfully passed without major incident, that I did eventually receive additional soldiers. This came about through speaking to the regimental sergeant major from the Port and Maritime Regiment. The new troops effectively formed an inner ring of security in the port, rather akin to the main castle in a motte-and-bailey fort.

Throughout my time at the port, I had to do whatever I could to attain successful results in our mission. This included requesting further equipment such as barbed wire and additional steel watchtowers.

These massive structures arrived on a huge truck a few days later—to this day I cannot say how they managed to get them to us! At low tide we created barbed wire defences; these reached down a small stretch of beach to secure one particular corner of the port. In some small way, it was a big achievement that helped me to continue ensuring that those two vital aspects of my leadership duties could be maintained.

Mission Four: Know Your Team

Your mission: to develop a strategy that will create high levels of trust within your team.

When these high levels of trust are present, then your team will be ready and willing to do all that you ask of them; they might even lift their masks for each other....

- What will you do today to start showing your people that you really care?
- What will you do tomorrow to create an environment in which your people feel safe?
- What opportunities are there for you to really connect with your team and get to know them on a deeper level?

Mission Four Checklist

It is often said that we manage things and lead people. It is also true that we would never attempt to manage something that we do not fully understand. To that end, if we are to lead people, we must know our people.

- There are times in leadership when we must hand control over to the team or to individual members of the team, trusting them to do their best for the team overall.
- Then, there are incidents when we need to take charge and command our teams.
- As leaders, we have much to think about, but we must always be cognizant of what those in our teams are thinking and feeling, especially in times of change and uncertainty.
- If those that you lead are to truly trust you, they must know that you know them. They must know that you care.

Serve to Lead

SOLDIERS CATCH SOME WELL-DESERVED REST AT UMM QASR

After a week at the port of Umm Qasr, I received a visit from my officer commanding, Major Tim Muir; a man I respected greatly as a leader and somebody I learnt many of my own leadership principles from.

Tim was a consummate professional who always made sure he emanated the air of a true leader. He maintained a high level of fitness, was immaculate in his appearance, and knowledgeable in every aspect of his role. He had a calm presence and somehow caused those around him to feel more confident in his and their own abilities.

He obviously cared deeply about those in his care and command, demonstrating this by balancing the needs of the mission with those of his men. He was always firm, fair, and inspiring; he also trusted me, allowing me to do my job. He would offer guidance when needed and held me accountable.

At this visit with Tim, I was given orders for my troop to rejoin my own squadron at a UN compound on the edge of the city. The journey back was a genuine relief, especially as I would be in more familiar surroundings. If only I had known then what was to come...

It was not long after arriving at the compound that we received orders to conduct a series of night-time house raids in the city. The strategy was this: my regiment would make simultaneous raids according to military intelligence, with the objective of capturing suspected Iraqi Army personnel.

When the war commenced, many of the Iraqi Army removed their uniforms and took to dressing as civilians. This caused a long and drawn-out insurgency campaign in which, for many years to come, coalition forces would fight and many would die.

The potential hazards that stem from not being able to distinguish civilians from insurgents were immense. When combined with the fear of risking one's own life, the mood was both sombre and exciting at the same time that evening, as I prepared to deliver my orders.

Essentially, my troop and I were going to drive into the heart of the city and at a specific time known as *H-Hour,* my Land Rover would smash through the steel gates of the house we were targeting and drive into the courtyard. We would then capture any suspected insurgents inside the house and secure the perimeter from the angry mob that was likely to gather outside, very quickly. We would then head back to the UN compound as rapidly as possible.

The orders I was about to give were the most significant I had given during my time in the army and I knew that not only would I need to inspire my troop, it was also crucial to instil within them confidence in me and my plan. As I made eye contact with them and prepared to speak, I thought of something that changed my perspective of what we were to face that night and I was propelled back to my training at Sandhurst.

The day I arrived at Sandhurst was the final step of a seven-year journey and the first of a whole new adventure. My decision to join the army was made at fourteen, and from there it had been a path I was dedicated to. From Army Sixth-Form College to Cranfield University under army sponsorship, I had set my goal and focused on it, until here I was.

As I arrived in my four-gear, red Ford Fiesta, with an ironing board shoved in the back, it was the biggest day of my twenty-one years of life. I could not quite believe that I was there, standing on the steps outside, dressed in my suit, full of excitement and terror. I knew that all being well, the next time I would be standing on those famous steps would be eleven months later on my passing out parade. I can still remember clearly the aroma of the building as I made my way inside; that unmistakable smell of the army, part history, part disinfectant!

The motto on the cap-badge at Sandhurst is one that I have incorporated into my own ethos and remains central to my leadership approach, both in and out of the army... *Serve to Lead.*

Servant Leadership begins with a natural desire to serve first. It is about putting the needs of others ahead of your own and making sacrifices for them. This is a conscious choice that creates the aspiration to lead.

This is in sharp contrast to those that aspire to lead first. Those who aim to lead first often do so because of a need to assert power over others, to increase perceived status or to attain the trappings of success. Perhaps the greatest difference between these two styles is that the Servant Leader seeks to ensure that the highest order needs of others are being served.

My first real example of this came during the first weeks with my regiment, just a few weeks after leaving Sandhurst. The entire squadron of around 120 soldiers were practising shooting on the Lydd and Hythe Ranges on the English South Coast.

The winter days were cold and wet, with a howling wind that chilled us to the core. This meant, by the time lunch came around, I felt absolutely wretched and ready for a generous helping of range stew. This was delivered in giant thermos-style containers, which tainted the food with flavours from everything that had been put in those containers over the previous ten years!

The squadron queued in a line with their mess tins and mugs to get their portion of stew and a cup of tea—also known as a brew, a wet or a hot-wet, depending on the military slang that was chosen on that particular day. Whilst technically it was tea, we often referred to it as coff-tea; another reference to the fact that the drink that came out resembled everything that had ever been in the container.

I had a sense that it was not right for me to be at the front of the queue, in the same way as many do not want to be first when a buffet is opened. So I lingered for a while, opting instead to join the line about three-quarters of the way back.

Within a minute of joining the queue, I felt a firm grip on my shoulder and knew instantly that this pressure was from a hand. Without even turning around, I knew instinctively that this hand belonged to a Senior Non-ommissioned officer.

My intuition was proved right, for as I turned and my eyes focused, I was met by the unmistakable face of the squadron sergeant major—a man who had probably been in the army for as many years as I had been alive. He looked me in the eye for a moment and then uttered words that have stayed with me since... these were another important leadership lesson.

Quietly and somewhat embarrassed, I moved to the very back of the queue and sure enough, at this juncture the two squadron captains and the officer commanding ensured that I was in front of them. This is how the army works and what it truly means to be a leader.

There is a very real chance that by the time one reaches the front of a lunch queue from all the way at the back, there will be little or no food left. Yet, this is the nature of leadership—to sacrifice our own needs and privileges for those we lead. This is because real leadership is not about the privileges that come with the role. It is about the duty and responsibility you have for those you lead.

The position of a leader is about what you give and what you give up, not about what you take. And, showing that you are prepared to sacrifice for the needs of others forms the basis of trust between you and your team. By caring more about the needs of your team than your own, you make those you lead feel supported and nurtured. They truly feel your intentions are to look after them and not to sacrifice them in favour of your own wants.

As we shall explore later, this duty of care goes far deeper and comes with a greater responsibility than putting your team first, yet this is a profound starting point. The importance of a leader using their time to do whatever best supports their team and their organisation is often forgotten in favour of doing what leaders do and having what leaders have.

A leader's job is to complete the task and look after those they lead. This can create a rather ironic disparity with corporate life. Those who would make the best leaders often forgo this progression in favour of serving others, whilst those who want to be served by other people find their way into leadership positions.

A real leader never believes he or she is better than those they lead; they never present an attitude of being aloof; and they never think that they do not need to partake in the duties of their teams because they are now a leader... Leaders are not exempt from getting into the trenches or getting their hands dirty!

There are incidences when it is critical for a leader to take a helicopter view of the situation, or remain in a strategic position—this is known as leading from behind. There are also times when they need to get stuck in, be it when things are going wrong, when the team needs it, or when the success of a team and the organisation depend on the leader leading from the front.

Leading from behind inspires confidence in a leader; it demonstrates competence and motivates those being led. Just as important, leading from the front creates trust and respect. It presents a very clear message that you care about your team and that you are prepared to fight alongside them when it is necessary. It crystallises your courage and compassion, your wisdom and your authenticity.

Inspiring all these experiences in those you lead is vital. My training at Sandhurst taught me how to inspire others; that it is not about being the loudest person —nor must you drain the room of life and energy. We all know what it is like to encounter a mood hoover who sucks any vibrancy from an encounter with them! No, you are aiming to leave everybody you meet with a greater sense of energy than when you met them. And you can achieve this in a quietly confident way.

People who know me often assume I am an extrovert by nature, because of how I present myself. I am actually introverted. Contrary to the popular misunderstanding, introversion is not associated with shyness.

Extroverts, such as my wife, glean energy by being in the company of others. After a week crammed full of meetings in New York, she will return home and arrange a full weekend of socialising with friends and family. This, to me, seems like Hell!

Introverts, such as myself, replenish our energy from within; by recharging in our own company. Time alone, such as a long bike ride, is essential for me after several days of events or meeting with groups of people. This does not mean that introverts are not inspiring. Some of the most inspiring leaders I have had the privilege of knowing are introverts.

The ability to gather the quiet confidence that oozes from an inspiring leader is derived from many aspects of behaviour and actions. This can be summarised as a need to master our state, from the position of language, focus, and physiology. Maintaining an air of calmness and stillness; how you stand, speak and generally carry yourself; what you wear and your appearance—all these are essential aspects of being an inspiring leader.

Many, many hours of marching up and down the parade square at Sandhurst and standing tall and straight as a die on my passing out parade taught me the physiology of confidence. The old army dress code of smart casual has stayed with me to this day—even on dress-down Friday in my corporate life I would have to look smart.

The number of times I have seen leaders in a really tatty old t-shirt and jeans looking like they have just taken them from the tumble dryer without so much as a shake! Now, I am not advocating a need to be inauthentic—I'm not saying don't be who you really are, but each of us does need to think about the impression that we give—in other words, what is your brand?

One particularly inspiring leader at Sandhurst was my company commander, who related his experiences of an operation in Kosovo. His squadron were being shot at by a sniper from a nearby block of flats and so he decided to send some of the soldiers to kick down doors and find the sniper. In that moment he knew that he had to lead from the front and be the man kicking down the doors.

There is an interesting distinction between leading from the front and the concept of micromanaging. I regularly advise managers and leaders to avoid micromanaging which involves always being involved in the detail. Here, a manager will tell their people what to do and how to do it at every turn, they will meddle, and generally want to be informed of each and every minutiae of detail.

A leader will make conscious choices about where they can be of best service to their team. They will ask how they can best be of service to their people, instead of solely looking out for themselves. This is something that I use at a level of unconscious competence and involves balancing the needs of the task, the team, and the individual. Many people will be familiar with these three components of John Adair's leadership model; which is perhaps the only leadership model that I recall from my time at Sandhurst.

As I stood in front of my troop, preparing to lead the raid that evening in Umm Qasr, I gazed directly into their eyes and decided how I could best serve each of them. It was only in that moment that I knew I needed to change my plan.

Suddenly I heard words coming out of my mouth...

And, with quiet confidence, so the orders went on.

"I WILL BE THE FIRST MAN THROUGH THE DOOR. AS SOON AS THE LAND ROVER SMASHES THROUGH THE GATES, I'LL BE OUT OF THE VEHICLE WITH THE SLEDGE HAMMER KNOCKING DOWN THE DOOR. ONE SECTION—YOU ARE TO FOLLOW ME IMMEDIATELY, ENTER THE HOUSE AND CAPTURE EVERYONE INSIDE."

Mission Five: Serve to Lead

Your mission: to complete a personal leadership audit.

If we are to demonstrate honesty and prove that we are trustworthy to those that we lead, we must start by being honest with ourselves. Answer the following questions as truthfully as you can, even if you are not entirely comfortable with the intelligence you gather.

1. As a leader do you seek to lead first or do you seek to serve first?

2. Putting the needs of others ahead of your own does transfer from the military environment to that of business. For example, do you give the first choice of holiday dates to your team? Do you demand that your team always plan meetings around your work and home calendar without affording them the same flexibility? Look at your diary over the coming weeks—what specific opportunities are there for you to demonstrate that you are prepared to put the team's needs ahead of your own?

3. Do you inspire those that you lead? Being an inspiring leader is about leaving all those that you meet with more energy than when you met them. Your final task in this mission is to gather some feedback. Identify three close allies from work and ask them for some specific feedback on how well you inspire others. Ask them how often they perceive you as positive and radiating energy and how often they perceive you as problem focused and taking energy.

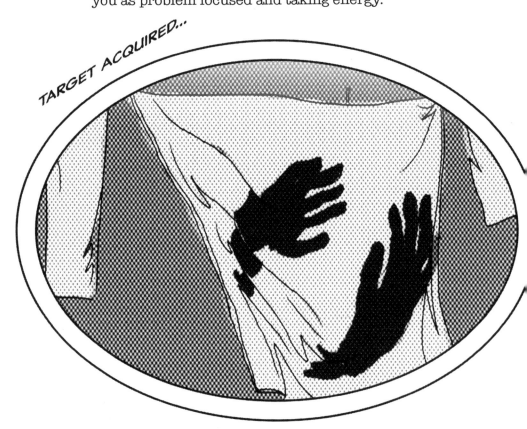

TARGET ACQUIRED...

Mission Five Checklist

When we put the needs of those we lead above our own we create an environment where they feel safe and supported. This, in turn, builds trust in us as leaders and enables us to make big requests of those that we lead. But it is not enough to just be trusted, we must inspire those that we lead to follow us and deliver our plans.

- Servant Leadership begins with a natural desire to serve first. It is about putting the needs of others ahead of your own and making sacrifices for them.

- By demonstrating that we care more about the needs of the team than our own, they truly feel our intentions are to look after them and not to sacrifice them in favour of our own wants.

- The ability to be an inspiring leader is derived from many aspects of behaviour and actions. This can be summarised as a need to master our state, from the position of language, focus, and physiology.

- The best leaders balance the needs of the task at hand with the needs of the team and the individuals within it.

UMM QASR, LATE THAT NIGHT...

Leadership Starts with You

The Land Rover jolted over a particularly large pothole in the road, reminding me of how much my body ached. I was so tired and disorientated as we drove past the mixture of concrete houses. This was the first time I ventured into the town and the mishmash of regular and irregular housing blocks was challenging to navigate.

We passed through slums and weaved along roads that were laid out in logic-defying ways. I checked the speedometer; thirty miles an hour. Each building flashed into view, gripped in the harsh light of the headlights, before being thrown instantly back into darkness as we passed by.

Desperately trying to decipher this unpredictable environment on a basic map was difficult. The task was made almost impossible by the harsh, bumpy road, which threw us about at odd, spine-jarring angles. I blinked to try and focus in the light of tiny a lamp that protruded from the dashboard on a flexible stick. I needed to stay alert!

The different areas of Umm Qasr had been given the names of towns and villages around Lympstone in the UK—home of the Royal Marines from whom we had taken over. Parts of the town were now called Topsham, Woodbury,

Farringdon and such like. All designed to allow us to understand where different units were and communicate easily without the enemy or locals knowing which locations we were referring to.

We sped along one of the main roads of the town, any vague points of reference flying past at such a rate than any hope of connecting what was being snatched away from my vision outside to what was being jostled around my vision in a blurry haze on the inside was lost.

I was in the lead vehicle of our small convoy, as we headed towards the house we were targeting for the raid. Passing a series of large housing blocks, I began to count down in relation to the map. I started speaking out loud to myself, "That's the first main block, cross a road junction, second main block, right, fourth house on the right on the next block. That's it there. GO-GO-GO!"

Suddenly my tiredness left me as the Land Rover pulled slightly to the left to get the angle for the turn then sharply to the right. There was a moment when all sound faded away, just the briefest silence before the storm came.

The next actions all happened quickly and instinctively—like clockwork. The metal gates burst open with a grinding crash as our vehicle smashed through. Before we had come to a halt and the gates stopped swinging, my door was open and I was leaping out with sledgehammer in hand.

Within little more than a second I had sprinted the last few paces to the door, trusting that the lads of One Section were right behind me. Never once did I think that they weren't. As I rained down the sledgehammer on the door, it crumpled beneath the blow and I stepped aside. In the next second the eight lads of One Section charged through the door behind me.

It is striking that on the night of the raids, I knew exactly what to do and did it... I led from the front and, despite the enormous risk, I was not overtly affected by the actual raids. I credit my extensive leadership training at Sandhurst for this—for it was not the action I experienced in Kuwait and Iraq that shaped me as a leader... it was my training and my values.

By the time I had stepped out of the Land Rover and into the house, I automatically knew what it meant to be a leader and how to be the most effective leader I could be. I knew when to lead from the front, as in these house raids, and when to lead from behind, as I did during the sniff test.

I knew my role was to lead by example (which does not always entail going first or doing things yourself). I also knew there was a fine balance between not taking unnecessary risks as a commander (putting myself in harm's way), and those occasions when as a leader I had to do just that and say, "Follow me." It boils down to integrity and knowing what it is to be a leader. It is about doing the right thing—not the easy or safe thing.

My parents instilled within me a deep sense of fairness and this ensured that at times when I could have faded into the background, said nothing and not acted, I actually did what I believed to be right. It was not easy and demanded courage, but I was compelled to strive for what was fair.

At school I was captain of my year's rugby team. Ours was not a successful team, even though we had some great players. The team in the year above had extra coaching during lunch breaks, which contributed to their success. I thought this bias in an opportunity to improve as a team was terribly unfair—I wanted to create a great team, so I visited the PE teacher to discuss this with him.

It was not an easy course of action. As I made my way to see him, my heart pounded in my chest, my mouth was dry and I had rarely known nervousness like it. However, I did it. I explained that it was not right for the team above to get advantages, which were not offered to all. I suggested that we also had additional lessons and, impressed by my forthright approach, he granted my request.

This was not the only occasion I had to go against the natural instinct for self-preservation to do the right thing. In my very first week in Sandhurst, I was having a bit of a rough time, as did all graduates of Welbeck College. I cannot say why this was, but I decided it was unfair and needed to change.

There was one particular lad from a very good public school who was throwing his weight around and being somewhat arrogant. Although he was bright and very capable, he would often talk down to some of my mates. I chose to visit him and explain my point of view.

That familiar feeling of heart-thumping nervousness remained as I walked to his room, but having made a habit of doing the right thing, not the easy thing, I could use past experience to focus on why I was doing this and not how it may turn out.

I spoke to him politely and was congruent by standing firmly by my own values at all times throughout the conversation. I said that it did not matter who we were and where we had been—we were all equals and in this together. I did not have a model to apply; there were no six steps to success that I could fall back on... I was simply clear and conscious of my values and acted in accordance with them.

As it transpired, we ended up being friends over the next eleven months at Sandhurst, with him going on to have a prestigious army career.

Doing the right thing, not the easy thing, is an important factor in being a leader, though it is one of various aspects. Appreciating how to balance the serving of your team, whilst looking after yourself is also essential to true leadership.

Leadership is not something you do... it stems from you and flows through you. Leadership starts with you.

Looking after yourself, to better serve your team is not about applying a model, it is about being the best you can be.

This was not always something I understood; during my stint in the Army Cadets, I embarked on a training exercise with the Territorial Army. It was the middle of winter, bleak and icy cold, and I found myself sitting in the back of a stationary, four-tonne truck. It was the depths of night and I stayed for many hours, until the sun began to rise and we conducted a simulated attack on a small town in the training area.

Being young and filled with a sense of infallibility, I could not be bothered to crawl into my sleeping bag, or make a brew. I just sat in the cold, without proper regard for my physical need to stay warm.

By morning, I had mild hypothermia and could not say where I was or what was happening. No leader can serve their team at peak performance when hypothermic and suffering from mild delirium!

It was not until my training at Sandhurst that I remembered this incident and truly grasped how a leader serves best when they are themselves healthy and fit. The army places a large degree of importance on physical fitness—regardless of which part of the army you are in. Clearly there is greater emphasis on physical fitness if you are an infantry soldier (compared to being an engineer repairing the navigation system on a helicopter), but physical fitness is not only important for carrying out physical duties.

The adage of 'a healthy mind in a healthy body' is very true, I have found. The fitter and healthier you are, the better able you will be to operate under pressure, the more you can cope with periods of stress, make decisions under pressure, and cope with a lack of sleep if the crisis hits your organisation.

The only model I encountered during my training at Sandhurst, was John Adair's *Action Centred Leadership*. Here, three interlinking circles form a blueprint for leadership that focuses upon the individual, the team, and the task.

These core responsibilities are centred on achieving the task, leading the team or group, and supporting individuals. Whilst the latter is often viewed as being individuals within the team, I also believe the individual is equally applicable to you and your own well-being.

I now view this model not as something that needs to be applied to a situation or ethos, but something that can be adapted into a principle for success. So, looking after your own health leads you to serve your team better, so they can achieve the goal at hand more effectively.

It is important to reiterate that Sandhurst did not teach leadership through models; it taught us what it means to be a leader. My training instilled within me an appreciation for the great responsibility and privilege that I would have as a leader. This was not expressed in specific words or at any particular time— it permeated the ethos of the training at Sandhurst, and this is how I can best express it.

In my position as a coach and leadership consultant, my military career sparks great interest and I am frequently asked what leadership tools, techniques or lessons I can share from my time in the army.

I have reflected upon this greatly over the years until I had a revelation—so much of the leadership and management-development industry is built upon the application of models and tools. Do this five-step process and people will follow you... adopt these six behaviours and people will follow you... and so on.

This was incongruous to my way of thinking. I was seeking a model where there was none, attempting to articulate tools that would neatly summarise how to lead others. Apart from the Adair Model, I was not nurtured into leadership by tool or model... I was shown how to be a leader, rather than doing leadership.

Understanding the principles of leadership is akin to understanding gravity. We do not do gravity, yet when we fully understand it we can operate much more effectively within the world. For example, when engineers work from a position of understanding the principle of gravity, everything they do is done with this in mind. Understanding the principles of what leadership is and what it means to be a leader is no different. This means that we do not need to do leadership, we can focus on being leaders.

The difference between Sandhurst and the business world is that people join the forces wanting to be leaders. In the corporate environment, employees come with skills and passions in their preferred areas of expertise and are promoted into management and leadership positions. These roles are often accepted for financial gains or prestige, rather than the pleasure of serving a team.

In the house, chaos ensued with a cacophony of noise and motion; the people within were shocked and confused, children were screaming, the adults shouted and implored. We quickly separated the men and took them outside. They would be placed into our vehicles and taken back to the UN compound for questioning.

My soldiers began searching the house, and I attempted quickly to calm the situation down. I first removed my helmet to appear less threatening to the women and children. I instructed the soldiers inside with me to do the same.

Outside a large mob was forming, as we knew it probably would. We had no idea if they were just curious from the noise and commotion, or threatening. Either way, it would not be long before they became more hostile so we had to work quickly.

Through my interpreter I appealed to the women to tell me if there were any weapons hidden in the house. I explained it would be better for them to show us, rather than my soldiers ripping their home apart to find them.

A valuable lesson the army taught me, one that has served me throughout my career—when we face a crisis the best thing is to step back physically and metaphorically. This is a vital principle I have brought with me throughout every leadership role I have fulfilled.

During my Platoon Commanders Battle Course—a course that teaches infantry tactics to young officers—our instructor told us how to step back in the moment. In his memorable Australian accent, the captain recalled how he was taught, should he come under enemy fire, to find safety and then to take out his water bottle. Then he would drink half the water within—this would offer a little moment to gather his thoughts and decide what to do next.

In the increasingly chaotic situation that was unfolding in the house raid, it was important that I kept my cool and collected demeanour. As leader of my team, I needed to remain calm, reassuring, and clear headed. I needed to step back, whilst remaining engaged and fully aware of what was happening around me.

The next step of the plan was to secure the house and then contact the OC on the radio. He would then bring in the army search teams with their dogs. In the midst of the gathering mob, I asked my radio operator to send the message, "Objective secure."

Several very tense minutes went by with silence from the radio. And then the message came through... it was a message that made my heart sink.

"Ben, are you sure the objective is secure. I'm at the target house and all is quiet."

I had led my team to the wrong house! In my tired, disorientated state, in unfamiliar surroundings, and with so little time to think, I had given the order one block too early. The residence we were meant to be raiding was actually further along the street! I thought I had failed and was indescribably embarrassed.

Another few minutes passed of feeling terrible and I received the orders from Regimental HQ, via Tim Muir, that I was to move immediately to the original target house. I am grateful that I did not have much time to dwell on my mistake, before remounting our vehicles, briefing the lads on the new plan—which was the same as the rehearsal we had just done—and moved on to the target house.

In spite of my error in navigation, we had gathered some low-level intelligence and small arms from raiding that wrong house so my mistake was not entirely fruitless. I also learned a number of lessons that night from myself and the soldiers and officers around me.

After the originally intended raid was completed and unfolded in exactly the same manner as the last. I debriefed my troop. I put my hand up, admitted the mistake and took responsibility for it—without attempting to make any excuses. I believe that my soldiers valued that in me and the honesty I showed; their actions in the following months and year demonstrated the loyalty and respect that comes with trusted leadership.

Having integrity of mind and action is a vital aspect of being a leader. Being honest is the most important thing, above all else. I call this *The Ronseal Test*. Do your people know what's on your tin and do you deliver it? Do your actions match your words? Do you walk the walk as well as talk the talk?

On a cold, wet February morning when I was fourteen years old, I walked to school excited and nervous... today was going to be a momentous day. I ambled along, holding the legs of my trousers up, so not to drag my ankles in the mud; trainers on my feet, yet in the bag I clutched at my side was a pair of brightly polished shoes.

When I got to school I changed into my brilliantly shiny shoes and proceeded to receive the insults and laughter of my classmates throughout the day. I did not care about their actions or words, because today I would be attending an interview with an army major at the careers office at school. I was moving a step closer to my dream.

Later that day, I found myself sitting opposite the army officer, who asked if I read newspapers or watched the news on television. Clearly I did not, what fourteen-year-old boy reads a broadsheet paper every day? But in my teenage mind I thought I needed to, because this is what officers do. I replied that I was indeed an avid devourer of all things current affairs.

The major replied, "Great! Imagine I've been on Mars for the last year—what's going on in the world?".

I did not have a clue! In a single moment, I had undermined my credibility rather than own up to the reality and offer to rectify the situation immediately. As a leader you can undo all of your hard work if you are not honest—your hard earned brand, trust and reputation can literally be gambled away on one lie.

On that occasion I was lucky, as the officer in question gave me the benefit of the doubt and offered some crucial advice. He said to me, "Ben, remember that as a leader you don't need to have all of the answers."

This is the single most valuable piece of leadership advice I have ever encountered and one that I always share with groups and individuals. If more leaders appreciated this, a great amount would be achieved in a shorter time, and people would be more engaged at work.

When we understand that we do not need to know everything, we can let go of ego; release the notion that we need to appear invulnerable. Contrary to what some may think—when we do this people trust as more, follow us more willingly and feel more connected to us.

When I was fifteen, I travelled to the Regular Commissions Board or RCB as it was more commonly known. Essentially this was the army's assessment centre in Westbury where I went through a two-day assessment. This included interviews with senior army officers, written planning exercises, leaderless tasks (crossing chasms with planks and barrels), leader-led tasks and an individual obstacle course.

I set off on the train on my own, wearing my dad's shoes and a maroon sports jacket that did not quite fit. This was another step of my journey towards attaining my dream. Each time I moved nearer, I learned new things and applied what I had learnt previously. It was a long and at times arduous path, yet each time I placed another foot forward it meant I was getting closer and therefore, filled me with a sense of anticipation.

During those two days I was leading a task, which I was not quite sure how to complete. With the words of the recruiting officer in my ears, I knew I did not need all the answers—all I needed to know was how to get the answers I sought.

I asked my team for ideas, which they readily presented to me. Based upon these ideas I formulated a strategy and then briefed my team. I led the team to success, thanks to their input and the knowledge I gleaned from this.

There are times, of course, when you do not have the answers and there is no immediate means of obtaining help. One such occasion occurred on the very same assessment trip. We had to complete the Individual Obstacle Course, the outcomes of which I misinterpreted during the briefing.

Each obstacle on the course was described to us, but the brief was cleverly worded telling us what to do, but not how to do it. For the most part I was able to get through each obstacle I came to. There were, however, two that I struggled with.

The first was effectively a large slide much like you would see in any playground. The only difference was that the actual slide part had been turned into a tunnel by wrapping it in chicken wire. The brief was to get both myself and an ammunition crate, filled with concrete, through the tunnel. I almost did not make it, because the task of dragging the crate up the chute was very challenging; but I managed it with perseverance.

Comparing notes on this particular challenge with the other boys afterwards, I was discouraged to hear they had climbed the steps and thrown the ammo box down the tunnel. This was not the toughest part of the obstacle course for me... that came in the form of a seven-foot-high wooden wall.

At the time, I was only five-foot tall and could not make it over the wall as the brief had suggested. I kept running at the wall over and over again. Each time I failed to make it high enough to leverage myself over the top. Each attempt drained the energy from my arms and legs, but I kept going, regardless of the physical pain and exhaustion. I ran at that wall full-pelt, literally until my time was up and they told me to stop.

Feeling dejected and beaten, I returned home convinced that I had failed. It felt like the end of the world, as I told my mum and dad that due to those two obstacles, I probably would not make it into the army. Yet, I did get in, because the army was looking for determination as much as anything else. My struggle to complete those two tasks did not stop me from trying, and trying until I was ordered to stop.

Being honest about your lack of knowledge in certain situations or areas of expertise should never feel like failure. When you meet each challenge with perseverance and determination, when you are prepared to ask for guidance and take the advice of your team, you will demonstrate great leadership to all your encounter.

The honesty of their leader is the most important factor to a team—they prize it more than any other trait. This does beg the question, however, should a leader be 100% honest?

The Christmas of 2002 was a very strange one for me. At the time it was seeming increasingly likely that the British Army would go to war in Iraq. It was not definite, but my girlfriend, my family and I all knew that if the coalition forces went, that I would be going with them.

By early the following year, it was obvious that we would be deployed to Iraq and I began the heart-wrenching task of telling my family and parents, who were now divorced. Rather than explain over the phone, I met up with them individually, which meant I had to go through many goodbyes. I remember handing my father a brown envelope with my Will in it for him to execute should the need arise. I also recall in the final goodbye asking my stepfather to look after my mum. Two things that I had never thought about in any detail when I decided to join the army all those years ago.

These goodbyes were hard for me, but even harder on wife-to-be, who had to relive the experience as she came with me on each occasion.

We were given a date for deployment and I duly told everybody of this. The date was then moved, and moved again, and again. Eventually I stopped telling my parents and Jo that I was still in the UK waiting to go. I stayed in camp, letting them believe I had gone.

Whilst I was not in a leadership capacity when it came to my family, 100% honesty would not have served them well, as it just kept prolonging the emotions that were inevitable. It did not matter about me; it was their needs that needed to be put first—I did not want them to go through another tearful goodbye.

After the eventual, successful raid of the house in Umm Qasr, my troop and I returned to the UN compound. Once we arrived I headed to Regimental HQ for a debrief with Tim Muir. It was here that I learned another valuable lesson from the officers of the regiment.

I sat alone in a corridor of the rather shabby and war-torn Umm Qasr Hotel, drinking a cup of lukewarm coffee from a foam cup, waiting to debrief my operation. Going over the events of the night in my own mind, I was feeling a little stupid. One of the most common jibes that soldiers like to make of officers is that they can't read maps. I had proved them right and fuelled that particular fire!

Once invited to join the officers for the debrief, I was surprised that none of them; neither Tim, the intelligence officer, nor the commanding officer of the regiment, made any attempt to ridicule, reprimand, or make me feel stupid.

We discussed the operation, we made comments about the first raid, smiled and moved on. It was then forgotten—partly because we had other operations to complete and partly because that is what true leaders do. They do not linger on mistakes and they do not feel the need to put others down. They knew that I felt bad enough, so felt no need to say anything at all.

At my wedding, some three years later however, it was a different story! Tim took great pleasure in telling my mum (and anyone else who would listen), about the raids and my error in judgment. But I guess that all is fair in love and war!

Mission Six: Leadership Starts With You

Leadership is absolutely about putting the needs of others ahead of our own. It is about making sacrifices for the team as opposed to sacrificing the team for ourselves. And, at the same time, our health and well-being as leaders must be a strategic imperative. If we are not fit and healthy, in body and mind, then we are not able to serve those that we lead.

Your mission: to conduct a reconnaissance and then formulate a plan of attack.

The Reconnaissance:

Review your diary from the last two weeks, including what you did before and after work along with the weekends. How well have you done in the following areas?

- Exercise. Whatever that looks like for you—gym, dog-walking, yoga, etc.
- Food and drink. Are you eating well?
- Sleep. Are you getting sufficient, quality rest or are you burning the candle at both ends?
- Balance and relaxation. Are you constantly connected to work and technology? Are you making dedicated, quality time for family, friends and loved ones?

The Plan of Attack:

From your reconnaissance, identify three small changes that you can take starting from tomorrow. Once you have identified what they are, commit to them with the focus and drive that you would to raiding a house in southern Iraq. Set a reminder in your calendar, in your notebook, on your fridge, in your car—anywhere that will remind you to focus on this critical element of leadership.

Mission Six: Checklist

As leaders we will face many challenges both personally and with our teams and organisations. It is in these moments of challenge that the true leader we are, and are capable of being, really comes to the fore. Yet it is not what we do in those moments of challenge that defines us as leaders, it is what we have done in the easy times to prepare ourselves for the challenges ahead.

- Integrity lies at the heart of great leadership. It is about doing the right thing—not the easy or safe thing.

- Looking after yourself, to better serve your team is not about applying a model, it is about being the best you can be.

- Doing the right thing applies equally to looking after ourselves. In this respect, we must balance serving the needs of the team with taking care of ourselves, so that we can be at our best for them.

- When faced with even the most extreme of situations, we must take the time to momentarily step back—both physically and metaphorically. This provides us with the space and clarity of mind to think before acting. It provides the space to lead.

- As leaders we do not need to have all of the answers but we must have the confidence, humility and knowledge of our team that allows us to ask for help.

- Acknowledging and owning our mistakes as leaders, contrary to popular belief, strengthens our leadership position. It demonstrates our honesty and integrity.

- When we meet each challenge with perseverance and determination, when we are prepared to ask for guidance and take the advice of our team, we demonstrate great leadership to all we encounter.

Being a Leader

We stood in the desert, silent. Three black figures against the pale sand and sky, waiting. I watched as the two soldiers in front of me took a long, slow breath, their shoulders rising slightly as they inhaled almost to capacity. Then, with the passing of but the most insignificant moment, they each broke the seal of the masks and lifted them by just a centimetre.

It seemed like an eternity as they took a final sniff and replaced their masks. I watched intent and focused, seeking the smallest indication of chemical agents in their systems. These men had, on my word, put themselves at enormous risk; it was now my responsibility to act swiftly should there be any sign of contamination in their bodies.

In all my years of leadership training, there was nothing that could have prepared me for that moment. Since that one occasion, no test of leadership in a professional situation has compared to that degree of intensity. This was my trial by fire... my sniff test. And it is the benchmark by which I hold myself accountable as a leader.

In that moment I was the best leader I could be. In every situation I strive to be that leader. Whether in the military, my corporate experience, or as a business owner, I ensure that I match that level of commitment to my team (that I match that level of service), and that I match that level of care and thought to every person I encounter. Because you are always a leader, regardless of context or the situation—leadership is not something you do, it is something you are... and never stop being.

I returned to Iraq for a second tour of duty in 2005. Now I was a captain, serving a different regiment; second in command to a squadron of around 180 soldiers. By this juncture in the Iraq War, our efforts were focused on the counter-insurgency campaign. With the threat of roadside bombs and other insurgent measures, there was an edge of danger that made this tour very different.

I would be lying if I said that I was not afraid of the increased risk. Yet as a leader, my focus remained on the mission and my desire to serve my team was as fierce as ever. However, there were other considerations at this point—my life and priorities had changed. My now wife and I had become engaged and the wedding date was set before I knew I would be returning to Iraq.

Four-and-a-half months after my deployment, I returned home for ten days and in that time Jo and I were married. We moved into an army house in Abingdon—I left the officers' mess and Jo moved from her London flat. It was a busy few days; a brief glimpse of my life completely changing direction, before I headed back out to the Middle East to finish the last two months of my tour.

Suddenly, the risk of my being in a war zone was greater and more poignant than it had been before... I was now a married man and I felt I had more to lose. My lifelong dream to be a leader in the army and the time spent away from home, were now at the expense of something more precious to me. I became aware to a deeper extent of my own mortality and the effect my death would have.

If I were to stay in the army, it would mean further tours of Iraq and Afghanistan; a reality I no longer wanted as a married man. This presented me with a very difficult dilemma. Should I turn my back on the life I had invested my life in living, or continue to live my dream, even though it would mean long periods of time away from my wife and the new life that awaited me?

In the army, promotion to the rank of major is based on performance and readiness for the position. My experience was that below major officers tended to be promoted to captain as a matter of routine. Some captains then find themselves in very demanding roles as they were promoted based on time served rather than competence for that role.

During my second tour, there was one captain who was struggling with this. Their job was critically important to the regiment and their success. The lack of experience and the stress of being out of their depth, led to them making, what I believed to be, bad decision. This put soldiers' lives at unnecessary risk, which really jarred with my own personal values—and has continued to do so to this day.

As you have probably gathered by now, the care I have for my team is the most integral aspect of leadership for me; it is who I am. Experiencing another officer who was not best serving their team, in such a potentially hazardous way, was the deciding factor for me.

I was already 100% decided in my want to leave—for my wife and to give my marriage the best chance for success. This secondary situation cemented my resolve to leave the military. I wanted to look back and reminisce with kindness, rather than any negative feelings, so leaving at that time was right for me.

I had always enjoyed leading soldiers and being with other soldiers; a future in the army would have meant the eventual transition to a position managing things, rather than leading people, So, with this in mind, I decided that I could make a bigger difference in the corporate world. Here I could lead people within an office environment, whilst retaining a greater control over my own life.

A captain in my previous regiment had contacts in the company, World Challenge, which she offered me. Each year, she told me, they recruited a handful of ex-military personnel on a three-month-contract basis.

The role was to run the twenty-four-hour operation centre. From here 360 global expeditions were managed every year. The participants in these expeditions were schoolchildren learning new life skills, such as leadership and teamwork. As a dedicated leader, one of these contracts sounded ideal.

During my time in the army, I had embarked on many expeditions of my own and had a love of climbing, hillwalking, and mountaineering. I have climbed in ranges as diverse as the Alps and the Himalayas, as well as many other areas of the world. The chance to combine my hobby with a new career helping young people to discover the teamwork and leadership I was so passionate about, was one I grabbed with both hands.

So, I went for this job and I got it.

A determined and forthright approach is something that has helped me to attain success as a self-employed business owner. I've always believed that you create your own luck—we make things happen in our own lives. This was a lesson that my father had taught me from a young age and has remained a strong, personal value of mine.

I am not one to sit around watching a website for the ideal position to be advertised; I developed a strategy to get what I wanted. I made contact directly, kept in touch with them and did all that I could to ensure I was in their field of awareness when the next recruitment drive came up.

Leadership is not only about how you serve others; it is about how you approach every situation you encounter. A true leader will take a proactive approach to the circumstances they encounter to achieve success. Being a leader is about being a leader... at all times.

Walking away from my army career caused me to reflect upon the people I knew, the various circumstances I had encountered and what the future held for me as a leader and as a person. I was, and am always, grateful for that major period of my life invested in the military as a leader and in service to my country and my team—it helped to sculpt me as an individual.

Little did I suspect the future adventures I had yet to face, would fill me with a deeper sense of fear and challenge me to greater heights of achievement than I had ever known...

Mission Seven: Being a Leader

I am going to ask you to be a true leader, to yourself and answer some challenging questions. By answering them with total honesty and absolute integrity.

Your Mission: to compare your values to those of the organisation within which you work.

Write down your personal values alongside the stated values of the organisation. Once you have done this, consider and make notes around the following:

- Where do they overlap? The words may not be identical, but your interpretation may be. For example, one of my values is integrity which could easily align with honesty.

If many of your values overlap, you will find that in living your values, you are able to live the values of your organisation and be your authentic self.

- Are there any values that are in conflict?
- Can you continue to operate in your organisation with conflicting values? Can you really be your authentic self and the true leader you want to be in your organisation?
- Finally, consider this question:
- Are the stated values of the organisation the same as the values and behaviours that are enacted on a daily basis?
- If they are not, how do these actual values sit alongside your own?

Mission Seven: Checklist

In this final chapter of War Zone Leadership, we come back to where we began. We come back to being absolutely clear on what it means to be a leader and what leadership is.

- In accepting the role or position of a leader, we are accepting the responsibilities of leadership at all times and in all situations.
- Leadership is not something you do, it is something you are... and never stop being.
- As leaders we must be able to reconcile our personal values with those of the organisation within which we lead. Failing to act when we find that our values are in conflict with those of the organisation means that we begin to undermine our credibility and capability as a leader.
- Leaders must be determined and proactive. Leaders must have a propensity for taking action and making things happen. Luck and good fortune must never form part of any leader's strategy.

Covert Le

Top Secret

Section Two

ership

Covert Leadership: The Adaptable Leader

In a split second everything can change.

The normality and peace of a cloudy afternoon can break apart, shattered by a flash of lightning and the gut-wrenching boom of thunder that reverberates around your body. A simple, mundane task can unravel into a labyrinthine puzzle that pounds you with wave upon wave of conflict and challenge. A single word, repeated three times, can mean a terrifying, agonising death is just moments away unless you get that mask over your face before your next intake of air.

My eyes darted from the small screen in front of me to the clock. It was 4:15 on a regular Monday afternoon... but this was not normal. Something major was about to happen and every one of my senses was firing; telling me to throw myself to the floor and grab my kit.

A wave of adrenaline surged through my body; slowing time to the point where the clock seemed to stop and my thoughts sharpened into definitive action. The footsteps were getting louder... somebody was heading along the corridor towards me and I needed to act and act now.

My reflexes exploded into action as I propelled myself into an upright position. Without pause or hesitation I leapt across the full length of the room and slammed into the opposite corner, turning my body so that my shoulder took the brunt of the impact. They were at the door.

Not knowing if this was a colleague or an enemy, I cocked my rifle, tightened my hand around the pistol grip and pressed the safety catch. As the door handle began to turn, I inhaled once and then held my breath. Everything faded into an unearthly silence. The world stopped, except for a nauseating sensation of heat and itching that permeated my flesh.

The door creaked open and a dark shadow began to enter.

Resisting the urge to raise the weapon any further, I remained motionless as the figure stepped cautiously into the centre of the room. They were unaware of my presence and I noticed they gained confidence in their movement and pace. They reached my desk and then turned to face me...

It was Sally Jones from Human Resources, or Corporal Jones as I called her. As she noticed me standing in the corner of the room, clad in full kit, she jolted with surprise.

"Oh, Captain Morton! I didn't see you there... sir!" She cried hurriedly, stuttering slightly on the word 'sir', almost as if she had forgotten the all-important title and then quickly slotted it in before finishing her sentence.

"What is it, Jones?" I asked, relaxing slightly.

"I... I was wondering if you'd had a chance to sign off the contract I sent you?" She appeared strangely apprehensive.

I glanced at the neat pile of confidential papers on my desk.

"I was just about to read it," I said, gauging her every move and expression. For some instinctual reason I found myself squeezing the trigger just a fraction harder as if readying myself to shoot.

"I do need it by five, if possible, Captain Morton, sir."

"I'll see what I can do, Jones." I offered in a gentler tone. She smiled a sort of half-smile and then nervously went to leave. "Oh Jones!" I exclaimed in a louder tone. She jolted again with shock.

"Yes sir?"

"I haven't received this month's payroll data from the Finance department..." I began. "We will need to organise a surprise office raid to retrieve the data and interrogate the CFO. Can you inform the men?"

"I shall, er, rally the troops, sir." She spoke with an upturn in her pitch as if asking a question, although clearly making a statement. Something was very wrong.

Every fibre of my being bristled at her words. Suddenly the impulse was too great and I did something utterly unfathomable. I found myself raising my rifle towards her, towards one of my own. Aiming the weapon at her head, I could see the fear in her eyes. She took a step away and then turned, fleeing back down the corridor with a haunting wail of terror.

It may seem ridiculously obvious, but if you were to take pure military leadership from its context and apply it directly to the corporate world, you would very soon run into difficulties. Even though the stereotypical image of a sergeant major screaming at a row of worried-looking troops may not be entirely accurate when it comes to leadership strategies of the British Army, there do need to be degrees of adaptation.

These adaptations will ensure your actions are appropriate in an office environment, they will enable you to inspire those you are fortunate enough to lead. When applied consistently and authentically you will be able to ask those that you lead to lift their mask for you, metaphorically speaking of course!

It is important to remember right from the very outset that you are not just imposing a series of tools to the job at hand; you are seeking to create a paradigm shift in your attitudes and behaviours. Here, you are not simply changing the way you think leadership should be done—you are developing a series of new root habits and beliefs. These will alter the way you lead your team, department or business in an inherent and instinctual way that is fluid and adaptable to each context.

We could view this adjusted strategy as Covert Leadership. Modifying the leadership principles of the military and using them implicitly, rather than explicitly leading teams as a military commander. Honing in on each underlying principle and applying this to a very different context, you can be a leader, instead of just doing what leaders do.

As we shall see, simply applying a model is not an effective way of leading others—this is surface-level action that has no lasting impact (and may actually alienate your team because it is essentially inauthentic). Leadership needs to stem from your core ethos and the foundations need to be laid long before leading your team into the metaphorical battles of corporate life.

To achieve this, you first need to redefine what a true leader is and how the most successful leaders get the best from their teams. Most people confuse leadership with management; they picture a leader as somebody who takes control and dominates their team. This is not leadership.

This management style stems from ego. It boils down to how the glory of leadership makes the manager feel. Real leadership, such as I learnt in the

British Army, comes not from being the centre of attention, but through becoming the centre of strategic operation. A true leader does not strive for power, but for the success of each and every member of their team and the team itself.

To uncover how this is achieved we shall be investigating the leadership principles I developed during my time in the British Army, combined with my own leadership methods crafted over ten years in the corporate world. You will then determine how these can benefit your leadership approach in the workplace. I will share with you some of the experiences, triumphs and mistakes from my life to demonstrate how you can be the best leader you can be... not in some modelled or prescribed way, but in the way that is best for who you are as a person. In a way that feels natural, authentic and congruent to who you are, but the very best version of you.

It all begins with those confidential papers on my desk... for in those very documents, the secrets of Covert Leadership can be found. If you are ready to learn those secrets then join me in the next chapter of this story.

So, with a knowing wink to you, my reader, I place my rifle carefully on the desk, gather up the crisp sheets of paper, pull out the pin of a grenade and toss it into the corridor. And after a single momentary pause, I rappel out of the window on the thirtieth floor...

The Boss Who Micromanaged Me

"Hello, Mr Morton!"

The strangely Polish accent caused me to stir from unconsciousness. I was sitting in a very uncomfortable position, my arms behind me, hands bound together. An attempt to stand revealed that my feet were shackled to the chair.

"I'm so glad you decided to drop in uninvited."

My body ached and my mind was saturated with an uncomfortable mix of frustration and anger. I jolted my arms against the restraints, but there was no give, no escape. Becoming more aware of the environment around me, I could hear the monotonous whirring of a ceiling fan, blended with the resonant drone of a computer fan.

Lifting my head and gradually opening my eyes to the fiercely bright office, I fixed my gaze upon the woman sitting opposite me. She sat rigid in a huge, rotating executive chair and regarded me with a fearsome expression. I recognised her instantly... this was my arch-enemy, Meg Lomanya.

This grotesque figure stared at me through one milky-white eye, whilst the other, of piercing blue, darted erratically within the eye-socket; the pinprick pupil fixing on an object for a moment, before flitting to the next. Constant and unrelenting, the eye monitored everything, each detail and movement; it was paralysing in its omnipresent glance.

On her lap, she held a beautiful cat, with long, white hair. Yet, the sleek fur was wrapped in wire; each leg, the tail and body were imprisoned in the twisted threads of metal, rendering the feline motionless. Occasionally Meg would run her hand down the cat's spine, her long nails clattering on the cold wire.

That poor minion could only move if Meg permitted it, through the bending of a leg or twisting of the neck. This creature was as helpless and controlled as I felt in this moment—a puppet. This was the power of Meg Lomanya—to make all in her presence feel trapped, alone and out of control.

"Did you think you could just come here and coach me on how to be a true leader, Mr Morton?" She hissed. "Well, how wrong you are! You see, I have a master plan..."

As Meg Lomanya launched into what was obviously going to be a very long monologue, I found my train of thought wandering back to a point in my career when I felt equally bound by my circumstances...

I joined Tesco when it was the UK's largest business. With half-a-million employees and a strong international brand, it was the very definition of a globally successful corporate entity. With a business so massive, size was its greatest strength and its greatest weakness. As such, my time at Tesco was a period of intense highs and lows—a fact that causes me to reflect with a deep sense of ambivalence.

I learned a lot of profound lessons about business and leadership from some people and saw a stark contrast of how not to do it from others. I would often feel incredibly disappointed, even angry at times at how I witnessed some people in leadership roles behaving—they were not actually leading, they were micromanaging.

This lack of autonomy left me with an overarching feeling of frustration that ultimately led to me knowing I had to leave.

The predicament with any substantial corporate entity is that it is a very complex system that needs an enormous amount of strategic planning and maintenance to function. The sheer number of people, departments, business outcomes and goals is so vast that it takes pioneering big-picture vision, mixed with a perfect eye for infinitesimal detail to make it all work smoothly. Add to this mix the chaos of daily human behaviour and it can become a ticking bomb very quickly.

To compensate for the day-to-day failings of the system, large companies often create quick-fix solutions that become permanent fixtures in the way the business operates. Simple tasks can require an array of checks to achieve completion, which translates into the most basic jobs becoming cumbersome, restrictive and overcomplicated.

My experience of Tesco would frequently highlight these types of issues and forms the foundation for my feeling undervalued and marginalised. My role was working in the Global Leadership Academy to source and develop the online learning content. This information supported our leadership programmes and training around the world.

The sheer size of Tesco as an organisation required a degree of control and governance. In practice this meant that many projects could not simply be implemented—they would involve the writing of an initial discussion paper, followed by a period of socialising the plan. Then canvassing input and support, followed by the writing of a board paper, presentation of the paper and final approval (or not in some instances).

This drawn out, convoluted process went against my values and I struggled in that environment. In the army I had thrived on the Mission Command ethos, but here even the simplest of activities needed to be signed off. Responsibilities that were well within my capabilities always had to be run past my manager and every decision or action required approval from above.

I would regularly be assigned tasks, with what on the surface appeared to be a fair degree of autonomy, only later to have countless changes imposed. Often these changes were simply because I had not done something the way that my boss, or indeed his boss, would have done it.

It is not that I wasn't prepared to produce or deliver something the way that my manager wanted it done. The issue was that my boss repeatedly said that he trusted me and gave me a loose brief, leaving me to get on and do things in my own way; only to make changes when I presented the work back to him.

If we are going to give people freedom and autonomy to make their own decisions, we have to accept that they may do something differently to us. That is not to say that we cannot ask our team to make changes or suggest improvements to what they have done. What we cannot do is delegate the how, then demand that they make changes. That approach quickly leads to apathy and frustration.

Hardly any of the tasks I completed felt like they were actually a piece of my project or in my remit because of this constant micromanaging. My manager did not want to be involved in the detail, but felt that he had to be. I don't suppose for an instant, that the way I was managed by him was his natural style or how he wanted to lead.

I believe that he desperately wanted to lead in a similar way to my own ethos—there were many occasions when we discussed leadership; what it meant to be a leader and our experiences. We shared many similar viewpoints, although his style was very different to how he wanted to lead or would have done in another context—where the organisation's values matched his own and he could be himself.

He was not actively being dishonest or inauthentic as a leader. He simply could not be the leader he wanted to be within that organisation. Reflecting on it now, I suspect that he had many of the same feelings and frustrations that I had.

Complex corporate organisations can develop a culture of rigidity, where the processes and systems routinely take place under usual conditions, but fail when the unpredicted or unforeseen occur. When an inflexible leadership style of micromanagement develops in a company, it not only forms significant risk if circumstances fluctuate or change, it also causes issues on a daily basis for staff members who feel devalued.

Tesco obviously strived to create a better leadership ethos by providing training and development programmes. I had an encounter with a manager who had just completed one such course—his leadership development programme would see him promoted to a director position within the company.

One of the aspects of Tesco's training was to deliver a real project into the business. This would require managers to apply their learning and deliver through others. In principle, this is a great approach to leadership development. The problem that emerged with the translation into a real-life situation was that this particular colleague simply did the model he learnt.

The Tesco model—*Taking People With You* —was centred around influencing others. It was built on the concept of a baseball pitch which had four bases, or steps.

Base One, *Choose Your Attitude,* was focused on choosing your attitude and getting in the right mindset to approach the conversation or meeting.

Base Two was connecting with the person you are talking to and entitled *I See You.* It was designed to enhance connection between individuals, build the emotional bank balance and make that person feel valued.

Base Three was called *You Make Sense* which was about stepping into the other person's shoes and understanding what was going on in their world.

Base Four was *I Make Sense Too*—this was where you could make your request, explain your position or needs.

The model is a good one that is based on sound theory and solid scientific research. Where it failed to offer value was when it was applied rigidly, with steps one to three hurried and incongruent, so that people could get on to step four and make their request—or at worst, say what they wanted done. They would then expect immediate action from their team. They assumed the team members would be totally engaged because the steps had been completed and that was all that mattered.

In the particularly cynical corners of the business, on several occasions I heard people referring to the model as *Dragging People Behind You.*

On this particular occasion the manager in question approached my desk with a real sense of purpose and urgency. Rather than presenting a healthy attitude, he exuded a slightly anxious—I've got too much to do and not enough time to do it—urgency. He struck me as a man overstretched, who just wanted to get this meeting ticked off his list as soon as possible.

He approached my desk, said hello and asked how I was. He noticed the photo of my daughter on my desk and enquired if that was my daughter. He asked how old she was and before I had finished talking he had started asking me about my workload and what we were working on.

The alarm bells started ringing immediately. Here was a man doing leadership. Step two, connect with the other person, step three, understand what is happening in the other person's world, and so on.

I could hear a pause as he moved on to step three, see him thinking about it and virtually felt the cogs turning. It did not inspire me to do what he wanted me to do—I felt manipulated by him. Despite his efforts to put into action this influencing model, he just presented himself as a person that was very inauthentic.

This is what can happen when a manager attempts to do a leadership model, instead of being a leader. When a team member finds themselves trapped by the rigidity of micromanagement, combined with managers who do models, disillusionment quickly becomes apathy. Over a sustained period of demotivation, a team will either just do the bare minimum to keep their job or take their skills and passion elsewhere.

Prior to joining Tesco, I was extremely excited about working within a company about which I had encountered so many great pieces of feedback. I had read case studies on how they developed people and their excellent leadership approach.

Immediately and consistently, I was struck by the way Tesco hired many incredibly bright, talented and hard-working people. The calibre of individuals around me was so impressive, yet within six months I felt a deep sense of frustration, not only by how the lack of autonomy affected me, but also how many of those talented co-workers had been stripped of any decision-making ability.

At Tesco there was a definite culture of fear that permeated the organisation. Leaders were afraid of not having all of the answers when questioned by their managers. They were fearful of having strips torn off them by their boss. Why? Because they had already had a strip torn off them by their boss! Leaders would ultimately retain all decision-making for themselves, which ultimately led to everyone working a level below that they were salaried at.

For a while I attempted to work harder, to gain a promotion so that I could effect change and have a greater impact upon one small corner of the company, but my determination soon passed and I descended completely into apathy. Being micromanaged by my manager was one thing, but the culture of micromanaging was endemic throughout the organisation. There was a gaping void between the values of Tesco and my own.

You must be able to link a number of your personal values to those of the organisation you work for. If you cannot do this, or if one or more values are actively opposed to yours, then it is time for some soul-searching.

Are you and the organisation right for each other?

Mission: Leadership

If you cannot live your values and be true to who you are; if you cannot lead by being your authentic self, you will not be able to act with honesty and integrity. Your people may realise this is happening, but more often than not, they will be unaware of your challenges and just feel that you are not being genuine. When this perception develops, they will not lift their mask for you.

Over the fleeting period of eighteen months, I went from being excited about working for Tesco to simply going through the motions and doing what had to be done. I lost my drive to be the best that I could be.

Whilst there were some who naturally thrived in that particular environment and others learned to adapt to the rigid structure, there were many, such as myself, who could not reconcile their own values with those of the company and eventually parted ways.

The challenge is that even when some can function well in the inflexible culture of a corporate business, and others swallow their own principles to

survive, the company will ultimately run into difficulty whenever it encounters a volatile, uncertain, complex or ambiguous environment (VUCA).

When adapted for a corporate setting, the Mission Command approach of the British Army is conducive to success in a VUCA environment. Mission Command is built on high trust, enables flexibility and rapid decision-making, thus it empowers people to act

Tesco's rigid management style and by-the-numbers leadership approach meant that when entering a VUCA environment it experienced severe troubles. Despite being such a powerful brand, it has been unable to adapt to a changing market and ever-evolving world.

Meg Lomanya's milky-white eye continued to stare from within its dead socket towards some distant space, as the terrifying glint of the other eye became fixed upon me. Paralysed under its piercing gaze, I held my breath and waited in silence for her next words to be uttered.

"So, Mr Morton, you see I am in charge here!" She displayed an expression that was more grimace than smile. "There is nothing you can do to stop me from implementing my genius plan!"

As she launched into a bout of maniacal laughter, I reflected on the lessons I had learnt during my time at Tesco and how my military training could steer me away from similar situations. It had taken me so long to notice how unhappy I was in that environment that my wife realised long before I did. Before we can make changes, we first need to recognise that a change is needed.

I now regularly reflect on my personal values to help me be at my best and navigate the complexities of life. Whenever I feel out of flow or trapped in some way, I use what I call the *Personal Leadership Success System* to evaluate where I am and how my current situation resonates with my values. By reconnecting to my core values and using these as anchor points I discover the best way forward for me.

I thought about the principle of Serve to Lead... How the primary role of a leader is to provide leadership, not do the doing. How as leaders, we must put the needs of those we lead ahead of our own. And how the flexibility to lead from in front and from behind enables us to best know how to be of service to individuals, to the team, and to the organisation.

When you are consistently of service to your team, you are always a leader. Whilst some attempt to micromanage and control, a true leader is never bound or restrained by their circumstances. Whenever the unexpected appears, they have their own values to guide them and a team of empowered people to navigate the unknown with... people with their own expertise and talents.

Watching Meg cackle hysterically, I felt the restraints around my wrists and legs melt away. I was not bound by her micromanagement or attempts to control—in fact, it was her that was trapped by her own rigidity and need to do things her way.

"Well, I really must be going!" I explained softly, yet with assurance.

And with that, I stood up and walked calmly across the room to the door. The sound of Meg's wailing "Stop him!" repeatedly echoed behind me, as I exited through the door. Her commands, however, were met with no response because her disheartened henchmen were too preoccupied doing the absolute minimum.

CLASSIFIED

Mission: Reconnaissance and Retrieval

1. On a scale of 1-10 (where 10 is absolute clarity), how clear are you on your personal values?

2. On a scale of 1-10, how true can you be to these values within the organisation for which you work?

3. How much freedom and autonomy do you give to your team?

You're Always a Leader... Twice!

I twisted the last remaining pieces of wire around each other to form a contact and secured it with a small piece of electrical tape. There was a sharp clunking noise from further along the corridor that caused me to stop; frozen for a moment with my senses focused on the slightest movement or sound.

When I had determined there was nobody about, I pressed the button to arm the device. There was a moment of deathly silence, when I actually found myself holding my breath. The trap was set and all was ready.

I now had two minutes and forty-five seconds to get out of this secret bunker before the entire installation came down around me. I gathered my equipment and removed the fascia to a nearby air conditioning vent. It was then I felt a sharp pain in my left ribs and turned sharply to investigate the cause.

The cause was a six-foot-seven henchman with a crowbar.

Vent in hand, I mustered all my strength and swung the fascia above my head. It made contact with the henchman's jaw, creating a slightly metallic, yet hollow thud. He regarded me with a blank expression before revealing a disturbing grin. I was not going to get out of this in two minutes, ten seconds if I hung around to fight this thug.

So, I used my remaining strength to swing the fascia upwards, aiming for a different part of the giant's anatomy. There was a weird crushing sound like cutting through a cabbage; it even made me wince a little. The henchman groaned and began to topple backwards.

I did not linger to make sure he followed through with his fall to the ground... the echoey clonk, that reverberated around the ventilation shaft, told me my change of tactics had been successful.

I shimmied through the metal ducting and back out into the night air. The cloud-dipped moon helped me just enough to find my way along the rock face; my fingers seeking out minute cracks and clefts in the stone to hang my body weight from. I was grateful for what little light there was, enough to see the features beside me, not enough to see the drop below.

I made it to the ledge where my paragliding equipment waited, with just under thirty seconds to spare. I threw the bag onto my back and, without thinking, secured it into place. Then I leapt from the cliff face and into the black, gaping maw of night, just as the sky was lit up by the detonation that engulfed my senses.

The solid facade of rock that had been there moments before was now shattered into minute pieces and tumbling towards the ground below. The shock wave rippled through me and I only just managed to pull the release chord before my world faded into nothingness.

The barman gazed at me expectantly as I sauntered into the grand hotel bar, adjusting the cufflinks of my shirt and tugging gently on the tuxedo jacket. "Can I help you, Mr Morton?"

"I'll have a Martini, please. Gently swirled, but not overly agitated!" I smiled.

Once my drink had arrived, I wandered through the bar and out onto the balcony, overlooking the street far below. Embraced by the cool night, I looked up to the now cloudless sky, where stars above replaced the shards of granite that only minutes before had rained down upon me.

These were the same stars that reminded me of another time, another place, a different quandary to navigate my way through...

I was climbing in Switzerland's Saas Grund Valley, accompanied by two close army friends, Gareth "Cheeky" Arnold and Chris Brogan. We had completed our Sandhurst training at different times, but still we shared a common bond. It was this bond which had led us on many climbing expeditions together.

Those trips had forced us to push ourselves and each other; as friends we had experienced many close calls on some very tough climbs. And over the years we had become in many ways, a band of brothers.

We had all recently returned from serving in Afghanistan or Iraq and organised the trip to catch up with each other and process what we had all been through. For three days we had been up in the mountains bivouacking and climbing, before heading back to the valley for rest, food and to have a few beers.

Late into the evening, after too many beers and listening to too many Bob Dylan tracks, our conversation became a little more philosophical. We began talking about the army, our careers, what we wanted to do next—it emerged that we were all ready for a change. We loved our experiences so far; the adventure, being with soldiers, yet were not overjoyed about some of the politics and career manoeuvring that would inevitably come with our next roles.

Leaning against a fence in a Swiss campsite, I stared up at the stars that shone so vividly without any light pollution and chatted to my girlfriend on the phone. And from nowhere, a slightly drunk Ben came out with the bombshell—I was thinking of leaving the army.

I had always maintained that I would stay in the army for as long as I continued to enjoy it. My sights had never been focused on attaining a certain rank, such as getting to major or lieutenant colonel. Perhaps this was down to the fact that becoming an officer in the British Army had been such a long journey for me.

It was a decision made around fourteen, followed by eighteen months of selection process and waiting time, two years at the army's sixth-form college, and three years at Cranfield University.

This was followed by one year at Sandhurst and then finally, three months on a Troop Commanders Course. For me, this was subsequent to a further three months on my Infantry Platoon Commanders Course.

I had invested the best part of eight years working towards my goal. It was a lengthy road which offered me a long, long time to think about what I would do and how it might be in those first few days when I finally would become an officer and meet my troop.

Many months after standing there, slightly inebriated in the Swiss Alps, it occurred to me this was a pretty inconsiderate move. Jo had been by my side since I started at Sandhurst. We had met at my sister's wedding in Bath just two weeks before I started my training at Sandhurst and we had been dating ever since.

She had been there during all of the highs and lows, seen me at my best and my absolute lowest. We had stuck together through a long distance, weekend-only relationship for the best part of three years and she was, and is, brilliant.

And if that were not enough, she was the one who put make-up on me for my passing out parade at Sandhurst! My passing out took place just two days after a bout of drunken wrestling had gone too far. To this day I suspect that I may be the only man to have worn concealer to cover a black eye on my passing out parade. Perhaps it is no surprise that the inspecting officer that day did not stop to speak to me; he looked at me, spotted something was not quite right and just moved right along!

After all the support Jo had given me—the sacrifices she had made—I simply turned my back on the hard-fought future, drastically changing the path ahead for us as a couple and for her, all in a drunken, slurred message from Switzerland.

After that slightly hazy phone call, not much happened with my plans to leave the army. This was partly down to my contractual length of service after Sandhurst—I still had a full two years or so to go. There was little I could realistically do.

My desire to leave started to become firmer in December 2004 at 23 Pioneer Regiment's Christmas Ball. This was the regiment that I was posted to after Sandhurst and it had a real family feel. This unique regiment within the RLC was very special to all who served within it. During the Second World War it was its own corps; over a million men in size. We were part infantry soldiers, part engineers and part labour corp.

Jo and I both have fond memories of the two years that I served there and it will always be the best two years of my time in the army. I was a young officer in a regiment with a real sense of esprit de corps. The officers' mess was welcoming, Jo always felt accepted and one of my very best friends lived in the room opposite mine.

The ball coincided with my last week in the regiment as I was being posted to a training regiment the following January. That evening, on the steps of the officers' mess in Bicester I proposed to Jo and she said yes.

Whilst Jo never ever asked me to leave the army or even hinted at it, the thoughts reappeared in my mind again. I started to ponder my values and what was important in my life. I was making a bigger commitment to Jo; to our relationship, and I was uncertain if I wanted to go on further tours of Iraq or Afghanistan as a married man.

My impending change of circumstances was incongruous with the concept of heading to a war zone. So, whilst Jo and I were a couple during my first Iraq tour, the situation was now beginning to feel untenable—as if I had more to lose... and I was not prepared to lose it.

Upon reflection, this decision was very much a part of my own leadership style—there is a definite need for leaders, in many different contexts, to regularly re-evaluate their own values and to make decisions that do not compromise these.

My decision to leave stemmed from the balance between my career and my family. You see, I love my family, I love my work, and never at the expense of each other. This forms one of the guiding principles of my life and leadership.

Ten months later I was making initial preparations for my transfer to a different unit where I would be joining as the operations officer and squadron second in command. During a phone conversation with the squadron commander of that unit, I remember asking him what the regiment and squadron had coming up.

He replied, they were deploying on Operation Telic 6.

"Oh, are you?" I asked.

"Yes we are and so are you!" he responded.

In that brief moment a lot went through my mind... I can't possibly go, we're getting married in September and that will be halfway through the tour!

In the next moment... Shit, back to Iraq! It's different out there now to when I was there last. There's that horrible counter-insurgency campaign—roadside bombs, mortar attacks and ambushes.

My thoughts were thrown back to the desert in Kuwait; my body being jolted and contorted by potholes in the road, as we drove back from the Orders Group. Dusk was setting in and we were losing the light fast. There was nothing around us, except for the desert, the sky and the seemingly endless road.

Looming out of the eerie half-light came a Land Rover, stationary at the side of the road. A soldier in full NBC suit and mask flagged us down and before he had even reached the window of the vehicle, we were scrabbling to put our own masks on. He explained that the NBC dress state was *Three Romeo*—which translates to full suit and mask.

From the relative mundanity of the isolated road, we were suddenly thrust again into a frantic scramble to get into our kit. Adrenalin pumped as we desperately twisted into strange positions within the tight confines of the Land Rover, hindered by radio equipment, as we grappled with our suits, knowing that the very air around us could be filled with deadly chemicals.

Now, from the security of my office in Bicester, the memories of war seeming like some distant nightmare, I had more to lose and I could not face being there again. Putting myself in harm's way with more at stake than just myself... suddenly things began to seem very different with the world.

Nevertheless, *You Are Always a Leader* and cannot shirk the responsibility or accountability that comes with leadership. I knew that it was not only a matter of principle to go on that second tour of Iraq, but I resolved to do my absolute best for those in my charge—balancing their welfare and the mission were paramount.

Several months before deployment, I attended the very first meeting with 3 Regiment RLC, with whom we were deploying. I entered the conference room with my own officer commanding and heard the colonel of the regiment speak to his officers and NCOs.

"Here comes the enemy!"

Sadly, that moment set the tone for the next nine months. In part, because of the reaction it created in us, how we responded and how his regiment reacted.

And even more regrettably for the soldiers in my own squadron, it was indicative of the entirety of our time in Iraq. We were fighting two campaigns— one outside of the wire against the insurgents and one with the commanding officer and, whilst there were several members his team that I trusted, respected, confided in and developed friendships with, there were others who treated us badly.

Even when in the relative safety of the camp in Iraq, my soldiers and I did not feel safe. Safety is imperative to the dynamics within a team—when those we lead feel safe and protected they will do extraordinary things for their leaders.

I did what that commanding officer asked of me as an officer in the army. I respected the Queen's Commission that he held and I respected the command chain, but sadly I did not respect him. I found myself doing as I was ordered not because I wanted to, but because I was ordered to.

Once again, this did not adhere to my own values and I could not reconcile this situation—which ultimately was the final factor in my decision to leave.

At the same time I was thinking more and more about getting home and what I had waiting for me. During that tour I began to notice that I wanted to be with Jo and my family to a much greater extent than I wanted to be in Iraq with my soldiers.

I still cared deeply for my soldiers and was loyal to them with every part of me—so much so that on a few occasions it caused me to have arguments with other officers in public that I should have had in private. But part of me wanted to be elsewhere and I could not reconcile that with my values.

On 10th August 2005 I walked into the Adjutant's office in the dusty headquarters of Shaiba Logistics Base in southern Iraq and handed in my resignation as a captain in the British Army. The date was significant—it was four years to the day since I walked up the steps at Sandhurst on my passing out parade and it was giving the one year's notice that my contract required me to give.

"Another Martini?" asked a familiar voice that caused me to turn away from the stars. It was the bartender, who stood behind me with a certain air of regimented rigidity. He held a silver tray, upon which stood a glass of clear liquid.

I pondered his question for a moment; my nerves could use a second dose of that calming, numbing alcohol. All this intrigue and danger was a terrible toll when there is so much to lose. I regarded the shine of the skewered green olive that floated within those satisfying depths.

I swallowed and remembered my leadership values... then I heard myself saying, "No thank you."

"Are you absolutely sure?" he asked again, raising an eyebrow and half-stepping towards me.

"I'm very sure." I reaffirmed with a deeper, more commanding tone.

"Then, I'm very sorry Mr Morton, we shall have to do this the hard way!" In a single, fluid movement he flicked the tray into the air, revealing a revolver from behind his back.

I somersaulted away from the bullets that clipped my jacket as they sped past. Circling back into the upright position, I caught a glimpse of the silver tray descending once more. I launched into another somersault that enabled me to catch the tray and throw it, frisbee-like, towards the bartender. With a clang, the tray sliced the weapon from his hand, before embedding itself in the bridge of his nose.

His shriek of agony heralded secondary fire from an automatic weapon that came from some unknown source... this compelled me to leap from the exploding floor as the bullets rhythmically tore up the tiles at my heels. I leapt into the air and off the balcony of the hotel bar, falling into darkness.

In many ways my transition from the Army was an easy one. This was in large part due to the organisation that I joined and the specific job that I did.

Some would say this is luck but I do not really believe in luck—I think you make your own luck in life and we are all responsible for what happens to us. On the occasions that we are not, we still have a choice about how we respond and can accept accountability for our own actions. All of my successes or failures are of my own making, so for me, luck is a matter of timing and judgement and they are both things that we have influence over.

I joined *World Challenge* straight from the army, my job was essentially a high volume recruitment job for a youth development company. My goal was to recruit expedition leaders who would take kids on four-week-long expeditions overseas. The departure date for each expedition was set two years prior, so there was an absolute, unmissable target date for recruitment of these leaders.

The kids had spent those two years fundraising around £2500 each, so failing to recruit was not an option. This would result in the devastation of a dozen kids' dreams and it would have destroyed the reputation of the company.

When someone pulled out at short notice, the demands of having to recruit someone with the right mix of skills and experience were tough. I often found this more stressful than anything I did in the army. For whilst I did not face the same level of immediate danger, my success had such an impact on those young people's lives that it was sometimes overwhelming.

I loved my time at World Challenge because it was a great business with a great culture. Founded by an ex-army officer, there were several people in the organisation from a services background which helped me settle in.

We were not all in the same team, however there was an immediate sense of connection between us and a mutual bond that came from having all left the Armed Forces. Working alongside other ex-forces people made World Challenge an excellent career move for me.

There were many exciting challenges at the time due to the specific stage in the business life cycle. When I first joined the founder was still the CEO and the business was in a high growth phase (being prepared for sale in the next few years). We had also reached the point where the business needed to become more professional in terms of systems, processes and performance. All of this made for an amazing time.

In a slightly clichéd way, World Challenge had a real work hard, play hard culture—and we did both very well! It was a fun place to work, we all worked hard and there was a genuine sense of family. Leaders were close to their teams and teams were close to each other.

I got to know and love my team at World Challenge very quickly; partly through the nature of our jobs and the professional culture, yet also because I knew it was important to the cohesion of the team, so I did it consciously.

My team and I worked closely together, we had regular catch ups, one-to-one and as a team. This meant I was close to them, knowing what was going on and when. At times I would be doing the doing with them and at times I would step back, clear the obstacles, plan ahead and support them. All of which I could do because I had given them time—I knew them and their needs.

I also got to know them during time out of the office; at the countless recruitment and training courses that we would run, exhibiting at trade shows and company social events.

During my time at World Challenge, one of the parts of my job that I particularly enjoyed was running the training and selection courses for our freelance expedition leaders.

Each year we would employ around three hundred and sixty outdoor instructors to lead the expeditions. They would accompany the young people and teachers to perform two critical roles.

Firstly, they would ensure everybody's safety during their trek in the mountains, desert or jungles. Secondly, they were there to facilitate the experiential learning aspect of the expedition.

Therefore, we were looking for quite a unique mix of skills including mountaineering qualifications, youth work experience and knowledge of travel in the developing world. More than this, each expedition leader would spend four weeks with teachers, who were ultimately the clients of our business, so we needed them to be our advocates.

We ran a four-day training and assessment course for them. The first day-and-a-half was based at our outdoor centre in Buxton— I would often facilitate a large portion of this phase.

Upon completion of this, the prospective leaders would go out into the hills around Buxton with a group of students and their teachers, thus preparing for their expeditions. They would always be accompanied by one of our most experienced freelance instructors.

At the end of the first day of training we would take the potential leaders to the pub for a few drinks. It was never made clear that this was part of the assessment process though the shrewder candidates understood what was going on. Gaining an insight into their social behaviour and understanding how they would interact with a teacher for four weeks, was a key part of the assessment for us.

On one occasion, a particular candidate had caught my attention in that day's training. He had made a number of comments that raised an eyebrow— nothing particularly serious, just remarks that had piqued my interest. At the end of the first day of training, we told them which pub we would meet in and at what time.

One of our instructors, Stu, and I headed to the pub a little early to discuss the day's events, in addition to sharing our initial thoughts about the candidates. As we walked in and sat down, we both noticed the same candidate sitting at a table with a nearly empty bottle of wine.

My initial thought was that perhaps he had been drinking with a friend or another candidate. A few secondary glances showed that there was nobody with him and only one glass. I thought it strange, and was beginning to have some doubts.

As the evening progressed, the rest of those on the course arrived. Over the next hour or so he proceeded to drink several pints of strong lager. At this juncture he was getting louder and louder, saying various inappropriate things to other candidates.

Eventually, Stu discreetly suggested that I go and sit next to the man in question, as he was really drunk and starting to both offend and worry the other people on the course.

I duly headed across to sit near him to discover for myself that he was indeed, very drunk and behaving rather strangely. It was at this point I became aware of the body language of others on the course–they were worried. A few had also stated they would not be comfortable heading back to the centre if he was there.

Add to this, he was a very big man indeed; neither Stu, myself, or the two other members of staff were particularly sizeable in stature, so the thought of speaking to him was not something I relished.

Yet this was another of those leadership moments where I knew I had to act. I was the senior member of staff so I was accountable for tackling the situation. I quickly thought about support and who could help me... our chief instructor was a stocky fellow and he was local.

I phoned him but he was not at work that night; plus he had downed a few drinks at home so he was unable to come down. Back to me then.

I spoke to the landlord–who by now had become aware of the situation and wanted me to rectify it. When he next visited the bar, I followed him, saying to Stu, "I'm going to go talk to him. Make sure you're near me in case he kicks off."

At this point Stu turned to Rob, another instructor, and said, "Rob, Ben's going to talk to him, stay close to me in case he kicks off."

He did kick off!

Thankfully it was verbal rather than physical–he rained all sorts of abuse down on us, telling us we underestimated what he was capable of and we would regret it. At that point we had no choice but to call the police and keep everyone else in the pub until it was dealt with.

The police arrived, with Stu and I going with them to find and identify the candidate. A few minutes later we found him walking up the hill back to our outdoor centre. As one of the police officers approached him I heard the other one say over their radio, "Yeah, the guys were right. He's huge–you'd best send another car up before we approach him."

As a leader, you are always a leader.

We cannot pick and choose when we take on our responsibilities. We also have to ensure that we always do the right thing–even when it is hard or scary. This is what leaders do–they make the hard decisions; the decisions nobody wants to make. And, on some occasions, they have to put themselves in harm's way for the sake of the team.

Plummeting through the air, time seemed to slow to a point where each breath lasted an eternity. I winced as my foot struck a passing ledge, sending me into a free-fall spin. Light streamed from the hotel windows and whirled around my head, disorientating, leaving me unaware of which direction was up, which was down.

Suddenly I tore through one of the hotel's large awnings, which slowed my fall. Then I ripped through another, my slower velocity causing the material to sting as I passed through. Now, I was at least facing the sky, so I could decipher where up was... and more importantly which direction my impending death would be arriving from.

Before another thought could enter my mind, I found myself embedded in the final awning, ten feet from the pavement. The material had ripped, but not enough for me to fall through. Well, not immediately. With a strange, erratic tearing sound, I gradually bounced, wobbled, and sank through the material, managing to land on my feet, outside the hotel entrance.

Running my fingers through my hair, adjusting my jacket and straightening my tie, I was ready to make my exit, into the night and my next adventure...

CLASSIFIED

Mission: Reconnaissance and Retrieval

1. How clear are you on what it really means to be a leader?
2. How strong is the connection and sense of belonging amongst your team?
3. How safe and protected do those in your team feel?

She sat in a plush leather chair, rotating slightly from side to side as she regarded my entrance into the enormous wood-panelled room. She was leaning to one side her elbow resting upon the left arm of the chair; her head, precisely supported by the left hand.

As I walked towards her, I could see her covering her mouth with a curled index finger... she had something urgent to say and it was not going to be pleasant. She looked up at me without moving, no tilt of the head or change in position. This was not going to be good.

"Ms L." I spoke calmly, by way of a greeting and a sign that I was not apprehensive at her demeanour.

"Morton." She replied, mirroring my tone and delivery exactly. "Sit down!"

I glanced at the office chair on the other side of Ms L's desk—it was positioned so that whoever sat in that chair would be at a level lower than she was. This was quite a feat, for Ms L was only four-foot-two, yet still managed to be an imposing figure behind that hulk of an oak desk.

"I've called you in to find out where we are with these secret documents." She uttered the word 'we' with a particular pointedness, as if to emphasise that we were both accountable for my actions. "You have been investigating the information within them for several weeks now..."

"I've had a few setbacks. When undertaking these missions, I must be true to my own values..." I began to speak, but was silenced as the aforementioned hand came thundering down upon the desk.

"Stop!" She commanded. "I've been following your missions with interest, Morton, and as far I'm concerned, you are a liability. Firstly, you're captured by Meg Lomanya and then you destroy her secret bunker and then we have witnesses left alive in that whole Grand Hotel debacle!"

She paused for the briefest of moments, before continuing with her tirade.

"Frankly, Morton, we need people who are just going to get the job done—we don't need principles or values, we just need you to finish the job, regardless of the consequences!" She stared at me, deciphering my every movement. "You come in here with your New Age hyperbole and expect me to go all warm and fuzzy! If you're not the man to execute these missions, I shall have you replaced by somebody less scrupulous!"

"With respect, Ms L, my values are part of me—it is through my values I achieve the best I am able to achieve." I remained calm and focused.

"Yes, Morton—and I am here to ensure you achieve the aims of this organisation; I cannot be bothered with all this touchy-feely-airy-fairy, values-are-part-of-me nonsense. You are assigned to this task as a sledgehammer to a wall, and as with any sledgehammer you need to be effective through means of blunt trauma. If I wanted the surgeon's scalpel, I would get somebody from the diplomatic office to do the job!"

"Again, with respect, my role is not about dominating or forcing an outcome. My actions come from within me and are based upon my values, not how hard I can smash something into pieces!" I spoke with assertion, but never raised my voice or allowed emotion to interfere.

I felt ridiculed and undermined—I did not trust Ms L as a leader. She demonstrated no sense of respect for me or appreciation for what is important to me. As each word fell from her lips, her lack of integrity came with it.

"Your job is to do what I tell you to do and if you believe for one moment that I would have any compunction about destroying anybody who gets in the way of the mission, then you are gravely mistaken." She gulped for breath. "I would not hesitate to have you do whatever needs to be done to achieve the outcome I want."

I pondered her words for a moment... my mission was not simply to do at any cost, without regard for those around me. If I were to achieve mission success, it would come about because of who I am; my core values and how I strived to put those values into action. I could not simply bash away like some blunt instrument—I must remain true to my values rather than just do what she commanded.

During my time in the army, there were many occasions when I would talk about human resources with my wife, our friends and my family. They would tell me about the different aspects of HR and describe a typical HR remit.

The army does not have human resources under the HR label, so the view I developed was one of something pink and fluffy—as a typical army officer, I did not understand what I perceived as the soft stuff. In my view, it was literally a load of old rubbish!

It was no surprise that upon leaving the army, I would often tell myself that I was not an HR person. I would focus on what an HR Person did in their corporate role, most of which was wildly inaccurate and ill-conceived in my mind.

My ignorance actually hindered me from equating my army experience with that of HR.

As my initial contract with World Challenge headed toward completion, I was invited to apply for a permanent role within the company. This new role was positioned in the Ops Department of the business and would require the recruiting and training of the expedition leaders. These leaders would be skilled in mountaineering, jungle trekking and youth development; qualified enough to take groups of young people overseas.

My application was successful and I was offered this role, which I did for two years before being promoted to a position of even greater responsibility. Here I was running a second team, so in addition to the expedition leaders, I was now also recruiting and training all the employees for the UK-based expeditions and activity camps. I was now responsible for around 800 seasonal staff.

I was having a conversation with the managing director's assistant at the Christmas party. She explained that the MD spoke very highly of me and had suggested that I would be perfect for the HR director role within the company.

My initial reaction to this news was rather unenthusiastic. I had always put myself in the box of an Ops man and there was no way I would ever consider anything as tenuous and frankly, downright wishy-washy as HR!

However, many of the skills and attributes of an army officer, or any leader for that matter, are HR skills. Part of HR's role is developing others, taking care of others, making them feel safe, enabling them to come to work and be inspired to do their best. These are all HR skills.

If you are involved with leadership, you are involved with HR. I had spent the last three years doing a recruitment and training job—which in almost every other organisation would be positioned under HR.

After the party, I took some time to reflect. In the New Year, I suggested to Nigel, the managing director, that perhaps I should take on the HR director role. His reply was, "Great idea, Ben. I was thinking the same!"

In retrospect, it was probably Nigel's plan all along; to engineer my taking the role. What he could see in me—who I was and am—I could not see in myself, because I defined myself in a very limiting way. My misunderstanding of the fundamental roles of HR led to me perceiving it as something other than what I was in my career so far. It was not until I stepped back that I appreciated my core values and the overarching conventions of HR were essentially the same.

When my values and my skills aligned I flourished. I truly loved my role as HR director of World Challenge. The things that my beliefs drove me to do, were the things that needed to be done. So there was a symbiotic fit between who I was, what I did and what the job required.

My greatest successes in the army were getting the best from others, building great teams and developing team cultures. I genuinely cared about people and fundamentally believed that my role was to balance the needs of those in my team with the needs of the mission. This same finely-tuned balancing act was vital at World Challenge and this suited my style of HR direction precisely.

Values have always been important to me and have driven many of my big decisions in life—certainly around career choices. My decision to join and leave the army were both values led, as was my decision to work for World Challenge. Yet, when one's own values misalign with those of an employer, being effective as a leader or team member becomes extremely challenging.

My tenure at Tesco highlighted this, for ultimately, my personal values did not align with those I experienced within the culture of the organisation. Though the problem was actually more endemic within the business than simply in relation to my own values. The stated values of the organisation and the values that actually existed were incongruous.

Tesco was not a good fit for me and I was not a good fit for Tesco. Being completely honest, my time there made me miserable and I performed way below my best. However, at the time I could not see it for myself. And it was not until long after I left that my wife said to me, "Did you not realise how miserable it was making you?"

Our values can and do change.

As I joined Tesco my wife was pregnant and everything was starting to change. When Freya was born my own priorities also changed—what I saw as important in life became different. Until that point family would not have appeared on my list of personal values. My family have always been important to me, but now work and family balance is part of my core values.

This new-found love for Freya and my wife Jo made family even more important to me. It also deepened my connection to my parents, in a similar way to the bonds I have with some of my greatest friends from the army... Bonds that come from sharing extreme experiences.

If you cannot align your values with those of the organisation, then you cannot be honest as a leader. If you are trying to live and demonstrate values that jar with your own core values, then you are not being congruent as a leader.

If you are not being honest, authentic and consistent, your teams, clients and customers will see through you and will not be inclined to follow you. They may work for you, they may do as you ask, but they will not go the extra mile for you—they will not lift their mask for you.

If you cannot align your values with those of the organisation, then it may be time for you to move on. You do not need to align every single one of your values, but you need to have significant alignment for the relationship to work.

If there is a major clash of values that you cannot reconcile, it may be time to move on for the sake of you, your family, your colleagues and team. This is how it was for me at Tesco, because if I was not looking after myself by remaining true to my values, I could not lead and look after others.

When we talk of aligning our personal values to the stated values of the organisation for which we work, it is important to be clear that the sentiment is what we are seeking to align. If we attempted simply to align the values word for word—akin to a game of Values Snap—we would be unlikely to find many organisations that were a match.

The key element is to understand what your core values mean to you; appreciating what the organisation's values are in practice. For instance, a crucial reason that I chose to work with my friends and colleagues at *TwentyOne Leadership* was that I could see, from their actions, that we shared a number of core values and beliefs.

When joining the team at TwentyOne Leadership, these were implicit beliefs. The team at the time consisted of Richard Nugent and Brian Lumsdon. Whilst there were no publicised organisational values for the business, it was clear to me what they both believed in, how this impacted relationships with clients and the values the business was being built upon.

Not long after I joined the team we sat together, investing time exploring our personal values, what the words we chose to describe these values actually meant to us and where there was a crossover. It was from this exercise, and investing time in sharing our core values, that the values of TwentyOne Leadership were born. Our values of honesty, connection, balance, energy and innovation.

My personal values align very closely to those of the business, despite the fact that only two of the actual words are the same. The word *honesty* does not feature in my list of five personal values—I use integrity. However, my definition of integrity aligns, in practice, with Richard and Brian's definition of honesty. The words may not be the same but the personal meaning is very close.

"I have an assignment for you, Morton!" Ms L barked as she slid towards me across the expanse of desk, a beige folder. I noticed the words *Top Secret* emblazoned across it in a faded red ink. "I want you to complete this mission at any cost."

I took the file and, as if to show willing, I flicked through the pages without really paying attention. My thoughts remained with my own introspection on values. I needed to be who I was, to be driven to action from my own values, just to be—and let doing do.

"That'll be all!" she exclaimed, implicitly requesting that I leave.

I stood and paused, wondering if I should say something to her, but decided against that course of action. Instead, I favoured the approach of retreat. Turning on my heels and walking towards the door; not even stopping to acknowledge Ms L's final threat...

"Oh, and Morton—bring on the blunt trauma. This is your last chance to show me your worth." Her words echoed behind me as I swung open the door and stepped into the new adventure, beyond...

Mission: Reconnaissance and Retrieval

1. How closely aligned are your personal values to those of the organisation for which you work or lead?

2. How closely aligned are your personal values to the specific role that you take in the organisation?

3. How often are your values and the organisation's values used as the check and balance for making difficult decisions?

What impact is all of the above having on your ability to lead?

Golden Lie

The vague flash of random branches passed my face as I wove through the forest. Ducking under the thick bough of an old tree, scuffing my arm against the rough trunk of a palm, then leaping over a contorted patch of undergrowth.

My heart was pounding in my chest, the surrounding environment began to blur—my situation was looking grim. The truth serum was taking hold of my central nervous system and my only hope of getting out of this situation was to evade capture. If my pursuers caught up with me now, I would be unable to lie.

I had managed to infiltrate a secret encampment of the evil genius, Scary Manager. Once in the camp, I uncovered a dossier about his clandestine research into truth serums and the nature of extracting an honest response from those being interrogated.

I knew Scary Manager had been conducting tests in this area, but what completely blindsided me was a paper on the *Golden Lie*—a concoction of neurotoxins that made people tell lies. The reasoning behind this horrific chemical mix; if everybody was made to lie to each other, it would undermine trust.

A world without trust would dissolve the very fibres of leadership and community structure. Families would argue, professional teams would fail to get the results they needed and businesses would collapse.

The undermining of truth was not as simple as it seems; for truth is at the core of authenticity... we cannot be genuine with others and ourselves without honesty. Honesty and integrity are the very fabric of business, leadership and just about every other aspect of a functioning society.

If the Golden Lie plans were put into action, the results would be devastating. Scary Manager would go to any lengths to keep them hidden from the world. Unfortunately for me, I had underestimated his security and was surrounded by his henchmen.

If it were not for a little sleight of hand, I would not have survived—in the confusion, however, I did manage to slip away, albeit after they had injected me with the truth serum. The same serum that was now causing the world around me to spin out of control...

At World Challenge, my military experience was invaluable. As an army officer I was ultimately responsible for the lives of others—a responsibility that I approached with absolute clarity and a deep sense of solemnity.

The entire team at World Challenge were ultimately responsible for the lives and safety of hundreds of young people on expeditions around the world. This sobering expectation was a constant, as we balanced the goals of developing them as people, whilst making a profit in the process.

This mix of aims and priorities required leaders with integrity; leaders who were capable of making the right decisions. I always maintained a conscious focus on the part I played in keeping these young adventurers safe—recruiting and training expedition leaders, whilst delivering the company's financial aims. Aims that were sometimes competing and required action with integrity.

My particular skill and values set was exactly what the organisation needed for that role—this was why an ex-army officer had previously been recruited in that same role by the founder and managing director, who himself was an ex-army officer. The integrity required with that degree of responsibility matches that of an army officer in very many ways.

This scenario typifies the competing priorities that many companies face—speed versus quality, whilst operating in an environment of scarce resources.

At World Challenge the scarce resource was people—partially the result of the organisation's previous actions.

Freelance expedition leaders were paid very poorly, they received their salaries late, we had not effectively communicated with them and made little effort to include them as part of our team.

Furthermore, we were never honest with them about salary amounts—deliberately avoiding the publicising of wages, as it gave us the flexibility to pay them how we wanted.

We strived to offer a little more than they had received the previous year, but there were many leaders with similar experience and qualifications being paid wildly different amounts, and they knew it.

This lack of honesty and trust eroded our ability to adequately recruit expedition leaders, whilst those we did employ, quite understandably, had little or no loyalty to the business.

This business practice did not sit comfortably with my values. On a more fundamental level, it was a false economy—impacting our ability to recruit, in addition to frustrating the teachers (our clients) with the service we delivered. We were plagued with dropouts, needing to recruit new leaders at the last minute, often at extortionately high fees.

It made greater sense for the company to pay leaders a little more, pay them fairly and to work towards eradicating the mistrust. Once I had completed a full year in the business, gaining experience and developing knowledge around the annual cycle, I proposed and implemented a publicised pay scale.

This was the key to solving the leader recruitment problem that had thwarted the business for many years. A solution, based in values and built on the principle that honesty and integrity exist at the heart of great leadership.

Strong leadership, combined with an approach rooted in honesty and integrity are the most effective strategies for the long-term success of any organisation. There are plenty of examples in the last decade where the opposite approach—one of dishonesty—has caused the downfall and demise of formerly powerful corporations.

This was merely one challenge that we faced—the daily battle to ensure high standards in safety whilst remaining profitable was ever-present. My team and I encountered various competing demands—priorities that meant the potential for wrongdoing, or a momentary lapse in integrity, was always near.

Checks and balances were in place within the organisation and these were fairly robust. We were the first overseas expedition provider for young people, awarded the various safety standards that were introduced in our sector.

Nevertheless, the risk remained. And much of our ability to mitigate that risk fell to me—a responsibility I entrusted to my team. Whilst I felt the burden of that risk and the well-being of the young people, the ultimate responsibility was with our operations director.

He was the one standing in a court dock if anything had gone seriously wrong and we were found wanting. If we had got it wrong, there would have been serious repercussions—financial, or in terms of human life. In spite of this, the trust and freedom he offered enabled me to perform at my best for my team, the business and our customers.

With monthly and yearly targets to hit, my team and I would receive financial bonuses if we were successful. This is a practice that many businesses employ to yield profitable results, however, poorly set targets and performance-related pay often drive the wrong behaviours.

We needed to recruit good quality expedition leaders who would keep the students safe, develop them as individuals and delight the teachers accompanying them—who were our ultimate clients.

Compromising on quality would only result in complaints at the end of the season, but still the client-facing team placed enormous pressure us to recruit leaders faster. Conversely, if there was a complaint at the end of the expedition it would not stop them from being quick to point the finger at us.

Should I give them any leader quickly, allow my team to get their bonus and deal with the complaint later? Or should I forgo my team's performance-related pay, suck up the relentless pressure from the School Support Team and give them the right leader when I found them?

This is a tough call when operating in an environment of scarcity—made tougher in the early years when we treated our freelance community badly and they had little incentive to choose to work with us over anyone else.

Often the single reason for working with World Challenge was: we were the biggest and our competitors had a strategy of only recruiting people who had led for us first. They would let our expeditions be a litmus test for recruits—which is not a great space to be operating in!

There were times when I had to stop, stand back and even sacrifice the financial rewards I planned on having when I took the job. I also made impossibly tough calls that deprived my team of some financial bonuses they had banked on getting when they took their roles.

Thankfully, with the value I placed on integrity, backed-up by the great team of people I had around me, we were never found wanting in this area. Through all this, I loved my team, so I later went into bat for them with the directors, making a case for them to get most of their bonus at the end of the year.

With so many outdoor instructors leading their first overseas youth development expedition with us, they would regularly make mistakes and learn a huge amount from this expedition.

After a leader's first expedition there would be a review of the expedition and notes would be made on the leader's file. When I came to assign that leader to another expedition the following year, the manager for that school would look at their feedback.

Understandably, they wanted the very best leader for that team, so would refuse those leaders with mistakes on their files. This could potentially lead to a director denying that leader any further expeditions. I always found this to be another tough, integrity based call.

I believed in developing the limited pool of expedition leaders we had. We were a youth development company–if I accepted this position and chose not to employ a particular expedition leader again, what would that say about our belief in developing people? What message did it send to our expedition leader community? And how would it impact our ability to recruit expedition leaders in the future?

If I made the wrong call and a leader repeated their mistakes the following year, not only would this reflect badly on me, it would damage our reputation with clients, the young people would not have a great expedition and it would impact our financial goals as a company. Another tough call.

At times, we also had expedition leaders work for us who clearly made errors of judgement. They either acted in ways that they knew were wrong or failed to conduct themselves as they knew they should.

These mistakes were made by expedition leaders who had worked for us for many years, with far more experience leading expeditions than I. They were better technically qualified than I was, plus they were well connected and influential in the expedition leader community.

With freedom in expressing their own version of events to their peers, many would believe them over us. As we had done so little to engender their trust, why would they believe us?

Additionally, we could never disclose the full details of why we were not working with that individual again–this would not have been the right thing to do, morally or legally.

As a team, we checked a leader's suitability to lead young adults; verifying their qualifications, first aid certificates and completing criminal records checks.

There was a hierarchy in place for the sign off procedure, though ultimately it was my responsibility—one that carried great risk if my morals or values were brought into question.

As leaders, our actions are often a result of our values. When we are faced with tough decisions, without a black and white answer, we must have a strategy; some decision-making process that supports us.

Operating in this grey area, my experience has repeatedly demonstrated that values help us make tough decisions. When we are clear on our values we can make those decisions faster. We can explain and defend them when needed, plus we can go home at the end of the day and sleep well in the knowledge we have done the right thing, not just the easy thing.

I awoke to the sound of a harpsichord. The environment was cool, unlike the heat of the jungle. My eyes adjusted to the room that gently rotated—I was obviously still under the influence of the truth serum. Blurred shapes moved about me and I could hear Scary Manager's voice as he barked orders at his heavies.

I was in a rather clinical looking lab, brightly lit with lamps and overhead strips of fluorescent lighting, yet the concrete room still seemed dark, dank, somehow claustrophobic despite its expanse. The music came from an old gramophone that crackled and wheezed through the melody of an old orchestral piece.

I heard the words, *Golden Lie*, and my senses snapped into focus.

With over twenty years of leading people and developing teams, I would say that trust is key to becoming a successful leader. Team members must trust each other—that they will get the job done and will not stab each other in the back.

Leaders must trust their teams to deliver; they must also give them the freedom to do so. Team members must trust their leaders to keep their promises, to look after them, to keep them safe, not to sacrifice their team members for their own gains.

Trust is a mixture of contributory factors that are so closely intertwined that it can be challenging to separate them. A major aspect of developing trust is honesty. Honesty can be viewed as being congruent, with your people knowing who you are and what you stand for.

The Army instilled in me a lifelong commitment to integrity—a personal value that I know will never be off my values list—integrity is being true to your moral compass; allowing yourself to be inspired to do the right thing, regardless of how difficult or unpopular it may be.

Another important element of trust is that it is digital, not analogue—this means trust exists or it does not. It is one or zero, on or off, people trust you or they do not. Trust is akin to a light switch, rather than a dimmer switch, so you cannot part-trust somebody, you either do or you do not.

During my corporate career a colleague and I were asked to travel overseas to give a big presentation. We would be presenting to some very important, key internal customers. If our trip went well, it would unlock the projects we were working on; that we had invested months canvassing support for.

Our boss would not be accompanying us on the trip, so gave us the task of writing and delivering the presentation. To best facilitate this, we asked for any specific guidance and tried to give her regular updates. The response we always got was...

...she unexpectedly asked to see the presentation with only an hour's notice... We presented our efforts to her and she said...

We both left the office extremely late that night and we both had families to get home to. This behaviour does not demonstrate trust; in fact our manager left us feeling incredibly frustrated and wondering why she had displayed such a dualistic approach.

In a complete contrast to this situation, soon after leaving the army, I had a manager in my early corporate career who completely defined how reciprocal trust can be and is achieved between a leader and their team.

He would explain to me what I needed to achieve and then leave me to deliver, trusting my judgement and my expertise in my field. As a result of this, I would have done pretty much anything for him.

Whilst he had never served in the military, he had, without even knowing it, mastered the army's concept of Mission Command. He would tell me what to achieve, provide me with the bigger picture (or why it was important), and leave me to get on with the task at hand. If there were some really specific elements that had to be done in a certain way, he would tell me.

For this approach, those words–*had to be done in a certain way*–are essential. Only brief people in specific terms, with rigid directions if results absolutely must be achieved that way. This is in stark contrast to wanting it done that way because it is the way you would do it; this is both demoralising and demotivating for your team.

The Mission Command approach is one of briefing and delegating in a particular way. It begins with explaining to your team what needs to be achieved. You then detail how this fits into the bigger picture and why they are undertaking the task. This is followed with any specific boundaries or limitations, such as budgetary requirements, deadlines, how this complements or impacts upon the existing work of colleagues, and so on.

Finally, you simply move out of their way and empower them to get on with the work in their own way, by figuring out the how for themselves. This process relies on trust and at the same time it builds trust.

When employing this approach you absolutely must not change their methodology when they feedback their progress, just because you would have achieved the results differently. You can challenge and develop their plan–this is what coaches do and is a really effective way to lead–however, if you are delegating the how you have to delegate the how from the beginning.

The Mission Command ethos works so well in the corporate environment, easily adapted from a military style. Each time you demonstrate congruency with this approach, you are stating very clearly that you trust your team–and they will reciprocate with trust in abundance.

Whilst I fundamentally believe that honesty and integrity are at the heart of great leadership, these traits will sometimes need to be balanced by caring for and being of service to your team.

This finely-tuned dance of care, service and honesty sometimes means that absolute truth is not always the best policy. During my two tours of duty in Iraq I was not always 100% honest with those I loved the most. I did not always tell Jo or my parents the whole truth and I am utterly fine with that.

My reason for having a clear conscience is because I did it with good intent, from a position of being true to my values and I wanted to protect them. I have also been honest retrospectively.

They now know almost all that I did during my time in Iraq. Either because I have imparted events to them or through my former boss, Major Tim Muir, sharing all at my wedding! And if they did not know most of what I did, they will do by the time they have read this!

It was during my second tour of duty that I was perhaps more sparing with the truth. This was for a number of reasons. They had already experienced the worry of their son and, in Jo's case, boyfriend being in Iraq eighteen months prior and I knew how nervous they were then.

The second time I was away in Iraq they managed—either through being absolutely glued to BBC News 24, or by taking the opposite strategy; attempting to avoid seeing and hearing anything. My relationship with Jo had moved on—we were due to be married, so had more to lose this time around.

It was easier to protect my parents and Jo during my second tour because of the nature of my job. As the squadron operations officer a large part of my role was planning the operations the squadron undertook. I also needed to control these operations from the operations centre within Shaiba Logistics Base.

My family vaguely understood my role so it was easier for me to tell them not to worry as I would be nice and safe in camp for the vast majority of my time in Iraq. This was not stretching the truth too much as this is what I thought my job would be.

However, once we deployed, my role developed to encompass responsibility for running large supply convoys to Al Amara, north of Basra. Al Amara was the most volatile operating area for British troops and came with a high threat from roadside bombs.

The year before my second tour (and the years that followed), we were essentially playing a game of cat and mouse with the insurgents.

They would develop a new roadside bomb designed to attack our vehicles. In response we would develop a new tactic, or piece of equipment, to counteract that device. This would be successful for a short while, until again countered by a new, high-tech, horribly lethal roadside bomb developed by the insurgents.

One such device was a bomb that was triggered by a beam of infrared light; this would be positioned to shine across a road. When the beam was broken by a passing vehicle, it triggered the timer on a shaped charge explosive. When the bomb exploded, it would fire a slug of liquid metal straight through the driver's door of the lead vehicle—the Land Rover—where I was often positioned.

We attempted to protect the occupants of our vehicles by strapping a canvas bag to the driver's door. In this we placed a number of A5 sized Kevlar plates, designed to fit on the front and back of our body armour or flak jackets. Unfortunately, this tactic proved to be woefully inadequate in negating the threat we faced.

As logistics soldiers we often were the subject of a lot of banter from our fellow infantry or cavalry soldiers. This would, on occasion, encroach into the territory of derogatory comments or scathing remarks where we became known as loggies.

In their eyes they were the real soldiers doing the real work of closing and engaging with the enemy—we were viewed as being somewhat superfluous. For much of my time in the army, we just shrugged this off as banter.

For most people, even those dishing out the comments, it came from a place of mutual respect. We were all soldiers, facing the same threats and all fighting for a common cause. There were times, however, when I encountered people who took it too far.

The convoys to Al Amara were conducted under a standard operating procedure. On approaching the outskirts of the town we would rendezvous with the infantry battalion based there. They would provide us with an armoured escort for the final 30-40 minutes into the town and their operating base.

These convoys were often conducted under the cover of night, so as we made radio contact to announce our approach, we would witness the road ahead spring to life. Lights would flare up, followed by the distinct rumble of the Warrior armoured vehicles as they pulled out of the darkness and onto the road.

Depending on intelligence and threat level at that time we would sometimes see the vehicle commanders, silhouetted against the moonlight, as they stood in the turrets. On other occasions they would be driving the vehicles, hatches battened down, and the distinct lack of a figure in the turret. This heightened the tension during that last, endless thirty minutes of the convoy.

After one such convoy, we rolled into camp and I headed to their HQ, ready to report in and confirm the details of our departure the next day. Whilst standing in their operations centre I overheard one of their NCOs making derogatory remarks about the bloody loggies.

Emotion bubbled over and I launched into a tirade in response to what I overheard...

"You call us bloody loggies and don't see us as proper soldiers!

I've just led a convoy of fifty soldiers and six local civilians on an eight-hour convoy!

I've driven through Al Amara in a basic Land Rover—nothing more to protect me and my driver than a couple of body armour plates in a canvas bag riveted to the door!

Meanwhile, you, the infantry, the real soldiers have popped out to escort us, driving armoured personnel carriers with the hatches battened down!

And we've done all that to bring you food, water, ammunition and concrete blast walls to keep you safe!

We all deserve a little more respect from our infantry brethren than that!"

Upon my return to Shailba I was duly called into our headquarters and debriefed on my actions. Their commanding officer had clearly taken exception to my outburst and had passed his opinion to my CO.

I took the dressing down on the chin, secure in the knowledge that I had done what I believed to be right and remained true to my values. I may not have expressed myself in the most respectful of ways, though I would not change a thing.

Did my parents and Jo need to know this at the time? Absolutely not.

Did I ever tell my parents and Jo that I had just led an eight-hour convoy to Al Amara in my letters and phone calls home? Absolutely not.

This is inherent in the role of a true leader—to protect and care for those they lead. I did not share these events with them because it was not in their best interests to hear what was happening at that time.

Essentially there was nothing they could do to help me, so knowing the reality I faced would only have caused more worry and emotional upset than they already faced.

Scary Manager was giving the order to begin shipment of the toxin. He had thousands of small glass bottles of the chemical to transport around the world; his agents were to use these on influential leaders, such as heads of state, business leaders and reality television stars.

I could not let him carry out his vial plan! The pages of *Hello* magazine are filled with enough mind-numbing rubbish, without making the celebrities lie about their latest trauma! I needed to act and act fast.

"Aha! Mr Morton!" Scary Manager's voice sounded like the crack of burning log; it was close and menacing. "I see you have rejoined us... just in time to betray your country and witness your own death!"

His words descended into maniacal laughter and the room continued to spin...

Mission: Reconnaissance and Retrieval

1. On a scale of 1-10, how much do you trust your team?
2. On a scale of 1-10, how much do your team trust each other?
3. On a scale of 1-10, how much do you believe your team trust you?
4. How well do you employ the Mission Command approach to delegation?
   - Explaining what must be achieved.
   - Clarifying why it is important and where it fits into the bigger picture.
   - Describing what the boundaries or constraints are.
   - Allowing them to work out how to achieve it themselves; whilst providing the appropriate level of support.

What impact is all of the above having on your ability to lead?

Mission Update:

By now you will probably have realised that it is not possible to answer the questions around trust on a scale of 1-10. Trust, after all, is digital rather than analogue. We either trust somebody or we do not.

If you rated any of the questions in this mission below nine or ten, then you and your team will benefit from an intentional and focused effort to develop deeper levels of trust, between team members and yourself.

Diamonds are Team Members

Brief flashes of light and shadow danced before my eyes, like the blur of soft focus on a summer's day, when the dappling of light through the leaves of trees meets the sparks of sunlight on water. I was disorientated, confused and thinking in moments—brief chunks of time, rather than a coherent stream of consciousness.

There were voices, questions, shards of noise that permeated my mind, but I cannot remember what I was asked or the answers I gave. I did not have all the answers, there were things I could not say or comment upon. I felt alone and in serious jeopardy.

I made out the silhouette of Scary Manager as he stood over me and attempted to force knowledge from me—I could hear myself talking about diamonds... ask the diamonds. He was getting frustrated and began flaying his arms around. A lamp overhead was thrust into an erratic motion, scattering light upon seemingly random trajectories around the room.

Corners highlighted, faces dragged from shadow for a fleeting second, before being obscured again, sharp edges, metallic glinting. I searched my thoughts, seeking the truths he wanted, but I had nothing to give—I needed the diamonds, for they knew the answers and could help me to make sense of this strange situation.

During my tenure with Tesco, I relied on my analytical skills—my focus was operations and the improvement of systems and processes, as well as the quality of the learning and development interventions.

I would watch as my boss invested a lot of time meeting people in the business. He would get together with them in the coffee areas, listen to the challenges that they were facing and share his ideas for aligning the learning and development activities. He would then come back to his desk and refine his strategy and the way forward for the team.

At the time I could not understand why he was so diligent about these meetings. To me it appeared as if he spent most of his time just talking and not doing the real work. On particularly bad days I would view his behaviour as self-publicity which felt very uncomfortable to me.

I would see this as networking which highlights how I had attached negative connotations to the concept of networking and, indeed, the word itself. Many have been led to believe networking is a negative thing; both sales-oriented and self-serving. Most people would describe themselves as being terrible networkers and hating it.

I had lost track of how important it is to know those you lead. In this behemoth of a corporate environment I forgot how the well-being of my soldiers in the army and my team at World Challenge had made us so effective. Whilst my boss at Tesco was not technically and hierarchically the leader of those he met with, he was absolutely leading.

He had a vision that he was striving to deliver and realised what I had misplaced—that as a leader you deliver success through others. Therefore, the role of a leader is not to do leadership, but to build, nurture and maintain relationships with their team and network.

It was not until after I left Tesco that it occurred to me how the style of networking my boss had perfected was not alien to me. This was identical to how I conducted myself as a leader—an approach that had served me well in the past. The only real difference was the context; the environment was the element that did not suit me, not the ethos of caring about your team.

In the army I was always aware of the responsibility placed upon me, and the duty of care that I had, for the soldiers in my command. As all had parents who loved them dearly, the impact of my actions extended beyond those that I led.

Now, as a father myself, I realise that being a parent is the biggest leadership challenge of all.

If the leader's role is to set an example for others to follow; to inspire others to be the best that we can be, then this is what we do as parents. Only as a parent there is no hiding from it—there is no downtime when you can switch off and relax.

This is why genuine leadership is so important.

As leaders we need to know who we are and always strive to be the best version of ourselves, instead of copying the leadership style of another or basing our leadership solely on models. By doing so, others will see through us or cracks of inauthenticity will tend to appear when we are tired.

And this is a common theme when we are parents, especially working parents—we often come home tired at the end of a working day, to use all our energy and patience on being the best we can be for them.

If we're not authentic, we start to behave erratically as parents. On one occasion we will say or do one thing. The next we say or do something entirely different.

As a parent myself, I make the same mistakes as many parents. I do not always get it right and have the exactly the same worries as most parents. I do know that, if we are not consistent, our behaviour sends confusing messages to young children.

Parents reap what they sow and this is also true of leaders in the workplace. If you are dishonest, incongruent and inconsistent, your team will not appreciate what you stand for and they will not completely trust you. If they do not trust you, they will not stand beside you and lift their masks when the day of your own sniff test arrives.

The jangling sound of machine gun fire in short, rapid bursts spattered through the air around me. I heard the air hiss in muted, momentary blasts as bullets whistled by my face. A man yelped in pain, a loud metallic clang echoed from beneath me and Scary Manager screamed in tormented rage.

A dark shadow completely obscured my vision, as what I now know was a person leant over me. I felt hands upon my arms and the tight restraints being released.

"Ben!" A woman's voice whispered close to my ear. "Ben! I'm going to give you the antidote... this may sting a little!"

I can remember thinking, "Ouch! That stings!" before the room imploded into sharp focus. The sound, light, and experience of motion came clattering into my awareness as I realised where I was and what was transpiring around me.

My tactical support team, the Diamonds, had witnessed my capture and were now here to help me. Without instruction or command, they had devised the best strategy to infiltrate the lab and initiate a rescue, each team member using their own skills to contribute to the overall plan.

They had entered the camp without detection, suppressed the guards outside Scary Manager's lab and launched a surprise attack to ensure my safe escape. Without their help, the outcome would have been very different.

I felt another member of my team help me up, I recognised him as Agent I. With a sense of resolve, he took my weight until I was able to support myself. It was now my turn to retrieve the dossier on Golden Lie, destroy the supply chain and get my team out of there safely. I took a deep breath and began to speak...

The hormone oxytocin is responsible for developing the bond between mother and child immediately after childbirth. The same hormone is also associated with increased trust, and reduced fear—which we know is crucial if people are to follow leaders.

When working within a nurturing environment, your team will naturally have elevated levels of oxytocin. Therefore, your actions, attitude and how you treat your staff through reward and displays of gratitude will have a major impact on how willingly they will follow you.

When a business is facing its toughest times there is a greater need to support and reward team members. If staff are expected to work really hard towards the goal of turning the business around, you need to show gratitude and support them along the way.

Growing shareholder value is not a motivator for many employees—there is rarely a direct link between this and the benefits for them. A great staff party, however, will very clearly demonstrate how valued they are. This is one aspect we achieved really well at World Challenge.

When I first joined the company, we would have a conference every two years for all of our staff. After a change in leadership, the new managing director made this an annual conference.

This change was a significant investment for our business, yet it was one that had huge value. The cynics would ask for (or even try to calculate), the return on investment of such an event, which is vast, but unmeasurable.

The culture and physical layout of the building at the World Challenge offices enabled people to sit and eat lunch together. This created a deep sense of connection, helped teams know each other better and enabled high performance. It also enabled me to make the transition from the army, by mirroring the closeness I had with my troops.

It is easy to dismiss this as insignificant—to remove the lunch and social areas from an office in favour of more meeting space, sales people or a bigger marketing budget—any gain from these will pale in comparison to a well-appreciated team.

The ominous rasp of a droning claxon sounded, urgent and unnerving. It heralded the imminent arrival of Scary Manager's henchmen, who would be coming through the lab doors at any moment. This brief moment of respite gave me time to further formulate my plan. Using each team member's individual talents, we would get each other out of this predicament.

The instant I was clear in my own mind, I explained the task at hand to my team and gave individual direction to each team member. I then got out of their way so they could do the rest.

I surveyed the room as Agents H and I collected the syringes of truth serum and positioned themselves beside the entrance into the room, ready to strike anyone that came through that door. Agent V searched for the dossier amongst the scattered papers that had, in the confusion, been strewn over almost every available surface.

The fourth member of The Diamonds, Agent M, was hunched over a computer terminal, having hacked into their network and was now tracking important data, downloading it to a data stick. An excellent multitasker, she also disabled the security systems, clearing our escape route.

Each member of my team was precious. They were all daughters, sons, partners and parents—to their loved ones, their lives were irreplaceable and their survival was equally as important to me as my own. My responsibility as leader was not to do everything, to micromanage them or do their jobs for them—I was accountable for their safety and well-being, in addition to inspiring them to use the unique skills they brought to the team.

Three henchmen burst through the door at once; I released a momentary burst of machine gun fire, dropping one man to the ground, whilst the other two were jabbed with truth serum. They both fell to the floor, clutching at their shoulders, where the syringes had been injected. The two team members by the door returned quickly to their position, ready for further onslaught.

"Sir!" Agent V called to me, "I've found the complete dossier, and this map with directions to the helipad... If we get there before Scary Manager, we can use the helicopter to leave!"

I instantly turned to Agent M, who was tapping away furiously at her keyboard. She paused for a moment before saying, "Sir, I can lock down the helipad and assign us a security code—that should keep Scary Manager and his people out!"

I agreed and as soon as it was done, my team and I left the lab behind, making our way to the helipad. As we slid along concrete corridors and through hefty steel doors, henchmen were rendered unconscious and any obstacle that hindered our way forward melted like butter before us.

As we approached our goal, we discovered Scary Manager and his remaining heavies attempting to leverage the door open with crowbars. Silently we crept towards them, until close enough to use the remaining syringes.

As Scary Manager fell to the ground, he was able to cry out one last threat before losing consciousness.

"No matter where you go, or what you do, Mr Morton... I will fail to make you pay for this!! Just you wait and see!" And I knew he was telling me the truth.

The door to the helipad swung open at the access code's acceptance and we headed through to the final challenge before freedom—there ahead of us, a sleek, black helicopter awaited us. As Agents M and V jumped aboard and prepared for our departure, my remaining team and I turned our attention to a huge stack of crates; each of which was emblazoned with the words Golden Lie.

I looked to my colleagues and smiled.

Mission: Reconnaissance and Retrieval

1. How strong are your relationships with your team members?
2. How strong are the relationships between your team members?
3. How strong is your professional network as a leader?
4. Have you articulated your personal values and leadership principles to your team in order to help them better understand and anticipate your actions?

What impact is all of the above having on your ability to lead?

The Guy Who Loved Me

Three thousand feet above sea level, I edged my fingers further into a crack in the rock. The sheer face of the mountain was a virtual wall at almost ninety degrees, though I was managing to cling to the minute surface flaws in the stone.

Occasionally the next practical fissure lay further than the reach of my arm, so I would propel myself towards it with my feet, trusting that I could grasp the chink in the rock and hold on. Once the grip of my hand felt secure, I could locate a new foothold and inch my way further towards the summit.

Below me the ground had now lost definition—what had been, merely an hour before, rivers, hills, trees and other landmarks had now blended into a kind of stippled effect, like oil paint on a canvas. My reality had become the small space of rock that I clung to and the immediate area of my next step.

Above me, blue sky blanketed my vision, arcing across the zenith, until sliced away by the crest of the mountain above.

This dark silhouette loomed over me like the impending bite of some ravenous maw. A feeling of dread came over me, cold and sickening... Ms L's words reverberated around my head.

"Complete this mission at any cost!"

After the debacle in the jungle, Scary Manager evaded capture and fled to the mountains. Once I had confirmed the safety of my team and delivered the uncovered data from the Golden Lie files, I continued to pursue the evil genius to his high peak lair.

This surreptitious hideaway masqueraded as a mountain retreat for the rich and famous—appearing as an exclusive boutique hotel and spa. Yet, behind the pretence of opulence and peace: a weaponised fortress.

Ms L's order, if I could not neutralise the Scary Manager threat discreetly, was to destroy the entire edifice. This would mean killing not only Scary Manager and his cronies, but also the entire guest list of innocent people who were simply there for a short break away from the limelight.

Was I prepared to exact a similar retribution on unsuspecting civilians, as I had on Meg Lomanya and her minions? The very thought of it put me at odds with my core values. However, in spite of my internal reservations, I continued the never-ending climb toward the top.

With each and every reach of arm and lift of leg, my mood became heavier. This mission seemed hopeless; I was ascending to a fate that would either see me sacrificed in bringing down a despot tyrant, or destroying the lives of many innocent people... What, in good conscience, could I do?

My introspection was cut short as I found myself staring at several feet of completely smooth rock. I scanned from left to right, but there were no finger holds to reach for, no cracks or crevices to grasp. I could launch myself up the face, hoping that the friction between my shoes and the rocks held me long enough to find a place to secure myself, but the risk was immense.

I stopped, slowed my breath and reflected for a moment on my predicament.

Striving for my best results at World Challenge, I found the high-pressured recruitment job was more stressful than anything I did in the army.

In the last few months before the expeditions departed I would stand in the shower each morning and feel physically sick. This was usually accompanied with chest pains and an intense feeling of not wanting to go to work. I dreaded my work phone, fearing that every time it rang, it was someone dropping out.

These were warning signs for me to change; to do something different. In that state of mind and health I was not effective. My overall physical fitness enabled me to cope, giving me the mental capacity to think and make changes, but only just.

This was significant for me as my wife lost her father when she was very young.

Whilst on the telephone to her mother, my wife Jo told her mum about my chest pains, of how I was feeling sick and stressed out by my job. She passed the phone to me and when I heard the tone and sense of concern in her voice, I knew she was deeply concerned. She told me that I really must look after myself.

Now at this point I dismissed it with "I'll be fine, I used to be in the army!" On reflection my response was quite hurtful and certainly inconsiderate. Yet, whilst I did not act immediately, that conversation was my catalyst to change.

Just as my Australian army instructor said—step back when under pressure. And this is a lesson that stayed with me through every leadership role in my career. Leadership is about others, but it begins with us, so to be an effective leader we must also look after ourselves.

You must pay attention to your own physical, mental, spiritual and emotional health. When you do this it allows you to think clearly when under pressure; to step back and see the bigger picture. Stepping back will highlight times when you are not looking after yourself, or perhaps your team, as necessary.

When the leaders we recruited for World Challenge expeditions dropped out at the last minute, we would sometimes have less than two days to find someone to replace them. Four weeks trekking in Borneo with twenty kids is quite the commitment, so this was challenging to say the least.

When each child has spent two years saving thousands of pounds for the trip of a lifetime, cancelling through lack of a leader was not an option—both for the sake of the Challengers, as they were known, and the future of our business. The pressure was immense.

On these occasions I would literally stand up and step back behind the bank of desks. Here I would take time to think. Our only option in these situations was to think creatively, then get on the phones and send out emails in an attempt to find a replacement leader.

The worst-case scenario was to determine who was departing in a few weeks' time and ask them to go sooner. This did not solve the problem, it merely delayed it, buying us some time and relieving some of the urgency.

Even in the most pressing scenario there came a point where we needed to go home. Remaining in the office until 8pm would not have made us any more productive. In fact, staying could actually hinder our overall ability, rather than help.

The best choice was to go home, rest and come back the following day, refreshed and ready to start again. This was hard, because I felt we should stay— or rather, part of me thought others in the business believed we should stay and get the job done.

Maintaining a good level of physical fitness and remaining active is imperative. Many people take up jogging, but you might prefer walking in nature with your dog or family—exercise is about what you enjoy.

I love riding my bike, to the point where I signed up for a big amateur cycle event called the *Etape du Tour* (Stage of the Tour).

It is a huge event every year where around twelve thousand amateur cyclists converge to ride a mountain stage of that year's *Tour de France*, a few days ahead of their pro-cycling heroes. The course is usually around 140km in length, including 3000-4500 metres of ascent in the Alps.

Although I had performed well in the event once before, I wanted to do better and ride it really strongly. I needed to train intensely, though I felt guilty about riding my bike during the day on weekdays. It just felt wrong, because I believed that to be successful as a professional, you needed to work every hour of every day.

To overcome this, I forced myself to train and created a set of commitments that prevented me from finding excuses not to do it. I wrote the event in my journal as one of the big five things I wanted to achieve that year and I told others about my goal so they would also hold me to account.

At the start of the year I scheduled bike days into my calendar and resolved to protect them unless something business critical meant I absolutely could not stick to them. I would take my phone with me, though if it rang I would look at who was calling and make a judgement about whether I needed to answer.

When I stopped for a break I would have a quick check of my emails and respond to anything urgent. Then I would get back in the saddle and defragment my mind again. This is akin to the process of Microsoft Defrag, where a cluttered disk drive is ordered, the index is redefined and useless data deleted.

I hired a physical trainer who was also a cyclist; I trained in the gym with him once a week, working through a strict cycle programme. Again, he was somebody else to hold me accountable for my success.

I did everything possible to achieve the level of fitness I needed; short of shutting down my business and moving to Tenerife to train at altitude for three months, I could not have done much more.

Eventually, I competed in the event really strongly...

Also, that year was the most successful and most enjoyable year I had experienced professionally. I looked after myself and got the balance right. The time I invested riding the bike and in the gym was not lost time—it was not time when I should have been at work. The training made me so much more effective when I was at work and led to being in a healthy position to succeed.

The notion of working long hours to achieve success is a myth that we have heard so many times that we've started to believe it. Now, when training for an event I ride my bike a lot in the week. And when I do, I have ideas and insights about the business and how best to serve clients of the business.

My thoughts of the daily grind are washed away, I step back and allow fresh inspiration to fill the space. My mind settles and I know exactly what to do for me, my family, for my team mates and for my clients. I am able to serve them better, and that is the true nature of leadership.

Most great ideas come when people are in the shower, walking for pleasure, or exercising in some other way, such as cycling, yoga, or in the gym. This is the same for people in New York, London, Sydney and most of the world! Our best ideas come when our minds are given the freedom to think; to daydream—when the clutter of in-the-moment thinking subsides.

As I lowered my foot onto flat ground and released my hold of the mountain, I gazed back at the descent I had just made. I had been no more than a few hundred feet from the summit and Scary Manager's clandestine retreat, but the price was too high. Not only would many people have paid too high a cost in the destruction of one crazed bully, but I would have risked too much in my own life.

Whilst I had always been ready to give my life for my country, the results of this particular mission would not have

been worth what I would need to give. So, I lived to fight another day... it was now time to look after myself and ensure that I was in the best state for leading others as I could be. In this instance I needed to be, the guy that loved me.

Mission: Reconnaissance and Retrieval

CLASSIFIED

1. On a scale of 1-10, how would you rate your work-life balance?
2. Thinking holistically about your health, fitness and well-being, where would you rate yourself on a scale of 1-10?
3. How good are you at giving yourself the time and space to think, on a scale of 1-10?

What impact is all of the above having on your ability to lead?

The Answers are Not Enough

Ms L sat at her desk, shrouded in darkness except for the bluish glare of her computer screen. She regarded the confirmation prompt before her and smiled a wry, emotionless grin.

Update Operative Status?

Her pinprick pupils darted from these words to the photo that was partially obscured behind them. She regarded the operative's face, his expression and then the agent's name... Ben Morton.

Her finger hovered over the mousepad as she overcame any resistance to her misgivings. And finally she clicked...

OK

The words disappeared, only to be replaced by another word, inscribed across the entire page and blotting out all semblance of the identity that had been there moments before. The word flashed repeatedly with rhythmic regularity; phasing into view for several seconds, then vanishing as if it were never there, only to reappear again as if to emphasise the irony of the circumstances.

Ms L sat back in her chair and regarded the word with satisfaction. This ominous harbinger of my fate...

ROGUE

Mission: Leadership

Being a true leader can often result in us underestimating the power of our actions. We will often demonstrate amazing wisdom, however, because leadership comes from who we are, it seems insignificant. This can create a situation where we devalue the importance of our own innate skills.

Many people who simply do leadership, and especially those who do it to stroke their own ego or maintain a sense of power over others, believe they need to be the master of everything to demonstrate how great they are. A real leader does not need to know everything, they just need to effectively leverage everything their team knows.

At Tesco, I spent a brief period overseeing the online learning resources; these supported the face-to-face leadership training within the Tesco Leadership Academy. For me, this time was a poignant reminder to understand where one's strengths are and how to align them with the organisation.

After twelve months in the role, it was becoming increasingly clear that I was not able to play to my strengths, whilst at the same time I realised my personal values were in conflict with the culture of the organisation. It was this realisation that led to me leaving the company.

As the last grimy carriage of the tube train disappeared into the tunnel with a howling, artificial roar, I noticed I was the only person left on the platform. Seizing the opportunity, I removed my mobile from my jacket pocket and flicked my eyes to the signal bar.

NO SIGNAL

On holding down the reduce volume button on the side of the phone for several seconds, a keypad appeared on the screen. I typed a series of numbers in precise order and waited as the phone beeped and transitioned through various screens. Eventually I received notice that a secure connection had been made.

NEW MESSAGE

I swiped my finger over the notification and the phone sprang back to life, dialling a series of numbers, followed by various clicks and whirring noises. After several seconds of abrupt silence a woman began to speak. I recognised the voice as Agent M from the jungle rescue.

"Ben, I hope you get this message in time. They're saying that you have gone rogue... all hell is breaking loose here and Ms L has assigned several operatives to tracking you down! I don't know what is happening but, Ben, whatever you do, don't come back to London... it's not safe for you here."

The voice descended into a loud click and the phone became silent once again.

I stood alone on the platform, frozen with shock. It took several moments to comprehend the impact of the message. What was I going to do? Where was I going to go? Was my family safe? Was I safe standing here on this empty platform?

The myriad questions fell away as the eerie quiet of the platform was broken by approaching footsteps. I dare not take the chance of leaving by the platform exit and coming face to face with whoever was coming my way. There was only one other means of escape, so before I had time for another thought, I found myself down on the tracks and heading into the darkness of the tunnel.

Whilst I looked after content for Tesco Leadership Academy, responsibility for the actual online system that housed that content fell to a colleague, Jane, in the same department of Tesco.

Striving to complete a major project that would refresh the system, we were involved in the creation of a site that was vastly more user-friendly in terms of aesthetic and user experience. This was not an area I had a great deal of experience in, although it was an essential part of the task at hand.

We were working with an external company to develop the system and had arrived at the stage where we needed to complete some testing—to use the correct name: User Acceptance Testing (UAT).

This basically comprised of checking every single page for content, typos, images or visual formatting that did not look right, in addition to testing every link on the page to check correct functionality.

Jane knew all about the system, however, she was away at that point in time, so the job of organising the UAT came to me. This was something I knew nothing about and whilst I had no competence in the task itself, I was competent in leadership.

As a leader in that department it was not my job to be the world's leading expert in UAT or even the system being used. I approached my role as an expert in leadership, so in that moment I fell back on what I knew best.

I brought my team and Jane's team together to brief them on the plan, outlining what needed to be achieved. This involved assigning a number of pages to each team, asking them to note down all the things that required changing, raising support tickets immediately with our supplier if an issue needed fixing and then making notes on the tickets raised.

We would then reconvene after several hours to review, repeating the same process until we were done. I also made a point of asking the team if I had missed anything or if they had anything else to add.

I was transparent in my approach, reiterating now and then that they had much more experience in this than I did, so I welcomed and needed their input. That level of honesty was well received by the team and helped us to get the job done.

I saw little point in bluffing or pretending I knew everything; I did not, hence this would have been inauthentic of me. This approach would not serve the team or the task—it was these two aspects of the project that I was responsible for.

In my time I have seen many leaders and managers take the opposite approach. They have either bluffed, failed to listen, or insisted on an approach based upon their limited knowledge of the situation. This is an approach that will always lead to suboptimal performance and undermine their credibility as a leader. ·

But what drives this approach from some leaders?

It often comes from a misunderstanding about what it means to be a leader. It stems from thinking that the leader is the most important person in a team. The truth is that we are not the most important person. Our role is to ensure that the task gets done in the best possible way and that our team are supported. Our needs, status and ego always come second to that.

I also made a point of thanking them for their efforts regularly, conscious of the fact that we were all working to the best of our ability and to a tight deadline.

In the army we had a phrase for this type of planning—*Troops to Task*. This is the simple act of identifying the work to be done and assigning it to the troops or people you have. If there are not enough people, you either prioritise, request additional troops, or both.

Barely able to see, I made my way through the tunnel, guided by the odd shadow or glint on the rail cast by the vague ambient lighting. There was an oppressive heat that was not warmth as such, more like a clinging, suffocating sensation in my throat and lungs. The overall blackness clawed at my eyes to the point where it felt unlike an absence of light and what I can best describe as an intense pressure inside my eyes and head.

There was a low, monotonous hum that permeated through the walls, seeming to get louder and louder the further I ventured into the void ahead. I knew I only had a matter of minutes before the next train and no way of escape if I were still in this tunnel when it came.

If those were agents, sent by Ms L to dispose of me, I would conclude that there would be more agents at the next station, awaiting my arrival. I could not go back, nor forward, and to stay here would be suicide. I did not have an answer for this predicament. Both trapped and lost, I needed to find the solution from elsewhere if I was to make it out of this.

Good leadership can also involve delegating tasks upwards to our own managers, and it was while I was doing just that for the UAT project, I caught the look in my boss's eye. It was a glint that told me he was confident in my abilities as a leader. As we walked away from the meeting together he gave me some feedback; he was really impressed by how I was running the project.

It is more important that we are competent as leaders, than being a functional expert. As leaders we are paid and expected to lead—not to be doing the doing. Furthermore, this tells us that as leaders we do not need to have all of the answers. I was not an expert in UAT, in fact I knew next to nothing about it. I was, however, competent as a leader, identified my weaknesses and understood how best to tap into the expertise of my team.

This level of openness and humility with those we lead is one of the most powerful methods I know for building trust. When we act in this way we say to our people, "I trust you enough to be totally open and honest with you." This inspires them to reciprocate the trust we have placed in them.

It also tells those that we lead that we value their opinion and trust their advice. It says that whilst I may be the leader, I know that you have the expert knowledge that I don't. I'm happy to listen to what you have to say and act on it. That is hugely motivating for those that we lead.

The erratic beeping of my phone gave way to the familiar sound of Agent M's voice calling my name with urgency.

"Ben? Ben is that you?" placing the phone to my ear, I replied that it was indeed me.

"Ben! What's happened? All hell is breaking loose here! Is it true you've gone rogue?" She sounded frantic with worry.

"No M, it's Ms L… she must have assigned me as rogue after I refused to take down Scary Manager." I paused for a moment, distracted by a loud clattering that echoed through the tunnel. "The collateral damage was too high, so I followed him back to London."

"You're back in London?" Agent M seemed surprised.

"Listen, I don't have much time…" I hurriedly explained my predicament and whereabouts, before asking for the team's help.

Almost immediately, I heard her calling across to Agent V and the rapid clicking of a keyboard commenced, reassuringly filling the silence created by breaks in conversation.

"We're just getting the original Underground plans up now…" Agent M's tone had shifted to what we referred to as her Mission Voice. The sound reminded me of the lab and coming round from the truth serum. "There's an old access passage, about two hundred yards from you. It leads to the street!"

I began moving, knowing I had barely any time left. Agent M explained that she would get Agents H and I to meet me at street level and bring me to the team, where we could plan our next moves. We needed to deal with Scary Manager and appease Ms L, or face hideous consequences.

The quivering of the rails beneath me, heralded that another set of hideous consequences had arrived a lot sooner than expected, so I lowered my phone and started to run. Seconds later, the glare of headlights filled the tunnel, illuminating everything around me. The sound of the impending train roared through me, confined to the tight space of the tunnel, the noise was all-encompassing.

To my left, just ahead, I spotted an access panel, which I assumed… I hoped, led to my escape route. I reached it and attempted to open it, but it was jammed in place, presumably locked from the other side.

The light of the approaching train blinded me; its thunderous scream ripping through my senses so it was unlike what we would call sound and more in line with a terrifying, painful sensation that caused my whole body to judder. I pressed myself against the wall and closed my eyes to the light.

Early on in my consulting career I was working with a manager from a very unique industry. At the same time I was working with managers in the department that she led to help them move towards being a really high-performing team.

The team had lots of challenges, lots of personality conflicts bubbling under the surface, issues with a lack of trust and a number of other things getting in the way of them being a great team.

The team leader, Louise, was a very competent leader and manager. She had successfully led a variety of teams before and possessed a great leadership track record.

The role she was moving into was leader of a very specialist group of people working in a real niche area. Her predecessor was a micromanager—a doer in the role, who was promoted to manager of a team of doers and then, eventually a department of doers.

This created a paradox in how the team viewed him—on the one hand they loved the fact that he had done their job previously. On the other hand, over time, it became apparent that some of his management practices were at the heart of many of the team's problems.

He had retained much of the expert knowledge, keeping it to himself, along with continuing to do much of the doing. This resulted, when he left, to things unravelling at lightning speed. By disempowering his team in the present, he failed to support them for the future; a key part of leadership.

When Louise started in her new role as leader, the team talked openly to me and to her about their frustrations—she had never done their job so how could she know what to do?

In reality, this was not relevant, because to be a great leader you absolutely do not need to have done the job of those that you lead.

When I was on my Troop Commanders Course in the army, examples of this came up a number of times. Instructing officers and soldiers would explain that on occasions we needed to put on a pair of green army overalls and spend time with the soldiers maintaining the vehicles. This may involve changing the oil on a four-tonne truck, changing light bulbs on a Land Rover or whatever task needed to be completed.

This achieved various results, because it allowed us to get to know our people and build a connection with them—a key factor if we intend to make big requests of them in the future. It also enabled us to appreciate their job and in doing so, we were better able to lead them. It helped them develop a sense of us understanding their job; what they had to do and the challenges they faced.

It was not our job to be doing that all the time or to become an expert in what they did, we simply needed to have a basic understanding of their job, whilst maintaining a mastery of leadership.

Leading is our role, not the doing—leaders look ahead, to plan, to anticipate opportunities and risks. Our job is to create the vision and strategy for the future and enable our people to deliver it. We do not deliver the strategy ourselves, we deliver through others.

Through my coaching sessions with Louise I concluded that she was pulled, psychologically, in two conflicting directions. On one hand, based on her personal values, she would be more than happy to put on a set of coveralls (they wore white ones in this business) and spend time working alongside her team. At the same time she was getting conflicting advice from her own manager—a leader for whom she had a great deal of respect; a leader who had previously led Louise's team. The advice from her leader was that she should not spend a few days on the shop floor with them; she had never done this herself.

Louise's thought process is a common one and it is also an approach to developing leaders that many take. There have been many books written and training courses delivered whereby we identify great leaders and attempt to replicate their behaviour and approach.

This approach can be a risky one.

What may work well for one leader will not necessarily create success for somebody else. This is due to a number of reasons. Firstly, the situation, political and economic environment may all be different meaning that what worked then, may not work now.

Secondly, the principles, beliefs and value-set of the leader we are attempting to emulate may be entirely different to our own. So, in practice, when we copy their leadership behaviours, these may not be congruent with who we are. Those that we lead will notice this.

To help Louise move on from this dilemma I asked her two simple questions...

"When your boss was leading this team was the situation worse, better or about the same?" Her answer was the latter.

The second question was, "And did the approach that your boss took have a positive, negative or neutral impact upon the team?" Her answer was again, the latter—it did not make things worse, but it certainly did not improve them.

Albert Einstein is widely credited for the quote, "The definition of insanity is doing the same thing over and over again, but expecting different results."

This rang true for me in this coaching session. Louise's well-placed respect for her boss was potentially playing against her in this situation.

This coaching conversation led us to the point where Louise was comfortable putting on a set of coveralls and spending a few days working alongside her team. When she really thought about it, this felt like the right thing to do for her and the team, plus it was an approach that sat well alongside her values. The team certainly respected her for doing it and it gave her a greater insight into the work the team did—she also got to know some of the team a little better too!

At any moment, I knew the train would be upon me, so all I could do was brace for the impact. The cacophony of sound became my everything and it was not until a hand grabbed my shoulder and pulled me through the now open access panel that I realised what had happened.

The train sped past, lights strobing into the highlight of the passage around me. I was kneeling on all fours, disorientated and my head still ringing from the clamouring echo as the train disappeared into the darkness.

As my senses calmed, I lifted myself to my feet and squinted towards my saviour. Virtually unable to recognise them, I leant against the wall for a moment, blinking to try and clear my eyes of their light-induced blindness.

"It's okay, Mr Morton, you're safe now!" The voice sounded familiar, but not in a good way—that accent was far too stereotypical to be friendly in a spy thriller.

I gazed towards the space where the voice had originated and gasped. My unlikely rescuer was none other than... Dr Know.

Mission: Reconnaissance and Retrieval

1. On a scale of 1-10, to what degree do you really understand the skills, knowledge and experience of those in your team?

2. On a scale of 1-10, to what degree are you tapping into this expertise and making the most of it?

3. On a scale of 1-10, how well do you do at recognising the work that your team do and thanking them for their efforts?

What impact is all of the above having on your ability to lead?

Dr Know

Standing in the shady confines of a cramped maintenance passage, deep underground, I faced one of my oldest enemies, Dr Know. I had encountered many dangerous people in my career; those hell-bent on destruction, power and bad management, but there was something truly terrifying about Dr Know.

His degree of intelligence, of cold logic, was somehow chilling. Whereas Meg Lomanya craved power and Scary Manager was just unhinged, Dr Know understood the consequences of his actions with an icy, emotionless logic.

His thirst for knowledge was matched only by his appreciation for the beautiful—yet, his scope of emotion remained purely in the realms of intellect and culture... When it came to compassion, the notion of serving others or caring about anybody, he was as dead to the world as one of the many paintings in his collection.

"Mr Morton," he spoke with a tone that could almost be interpreted as friendly.

"Please do accept my apologies for the somewhat brusque manner of my colleague here..." He gestured towards the hulking mass of bull-faced muscle that stood beside him—the owner of the aforementioned hand that had dragged me to safety. "...These were somewhat exceptional circumstances."

I said nothing, electing to nod my head ever so slightly as a sign of gratitude to the bovine creature that had just saved my life.

"I would imagine that you are wondering what I am doing here and why I saved you?" He did not pause for my response. "Well, Mr Morton, I've been tracking you for some time... you see, we have a mutual problem, which I think I can assist you with."

His eyes penetrated the darkness with a severe, quite petrifying glimmer. The sociopathic depths that lay within those eyes were veiled by an unknowable, inconceivable lack of empathy. The apertures of his pupils were so swollen, they caused the glint to seem much brighter than the level of light around us allowed. This gave the impression of a man who absorbed everything with inhuman voracity, yet gave nothing back.

"I have been called many things over the years, Mr Morton." He continued, "Maniac, despot, dictator... and I cannot say that these were entirely undeserved. I have done many unscrupulous things in my lifetime. Served my ego rather than others. Sought to control others with my power. I have even found myself in a bad mood and ranted about it on Facebook!"

I went to say that most people have done that, but again, kept my silence.

"However, Mr Morton, I am not an irrational man. My will comes from art, music, beauty. I am an aesthete, a lover of symphony and fine wines. I may use my inordinate amounts of money and authority to do what you deem to be bad things, but I am not a bad person—I simply value the courage to do what must be done, rather than the popular and dare I say, easier, course of action."

I reflected upon this, searching my own values and experiences of right and wrong.

"Unfortunately, there are those who are assigned the same labels as I; cases of appellation that are more, well, Appalachian." He chuckled to himself. "I believe you are acquainted with these individuals: the likes of Meg Lomanya, Scary Manager and Marcy Systyck."

I shuddered at the latter's name; I had encountered many villains in my time, but Marcy was in a whole other league!

"I appreciate that to you and your agency, we all seem identical in our will and want, but those creatures seek to create a world based on lies. I am an artist... and art is truth. In their world, all that I respect and value would be gone. So, Mr Morton, I am here to offer you my help..."

I have two main regrets about the period in Iraq leading up to my leaving the army. These are both directly related to my own values and my principles of leadership.

The first is that I did not do more to manage the relationship between my squadron and the regiment that we were attached to. In so many ways I felt helpless; feelings I would feel guilty about—we were part of the same army and the enemy was outside the wire, not within.

The other side of the argument I would have inside my head was suggesting that managing the relationship was part of my boss's job. He was the officer commanding, or OC, so that was down to him, surely?

Upon reflection all of those assumptions and thoughts were wrong—I was a leader and so my role, regardless of my rank or position in the command chain was to lead; to make things better. That was the right thing, not the easy thing, yet I failed.

I regret the impact my failure to act had on the 180 soldiers that my OC and I were responsible for. We could have done more for them—I should have done more for them. In this respect I feel that I failed in my duty of care as a leader.

Equally, during that tour, there was the regimental operations officer whose full competence I questioned. In that respect, I left with my head held high that I had done all I could to devise a strategy that kept my soldiers safe, whilst still completing the missions I was given. I balanced the two needs.

My other regret from that period was that I did not speak my truth.

Several weeks after resigning my commission I was asked to visit the commanding officer as he wanted to know my motivations for leaving. Two other captains from the regiment had also resigned and I suspect this had not gone unnoticed.

I walked up the dusty corridor to his office, knocked on the makeshift plywood door and waited for him to ask me to come in. As I walked in the door, I saluted and was invited to sit down. He immediately got down to business as he was a busy commanding officer on operations with a demanding job.

He asked why I was leaving.

I simply said that I had completed four years, enjoyed my time, but was unsure if I wanted to do the jobs that would inevitably come next. I continued, explaining that I was getting married and my priorities were changing.

He asked if there was anything else. I said no, he thanked me and I left.

I failed to speak my truth—I was not honest about my reasons and as such, I failed to act with full integrity. This was partially due to not wanting to make the next three months any more challenging for my soldiers. I was also aware that I still had just under a year left in the army, so was attempting to maintain a degree of ease for myself.

This was a sensitive situation though and the reality of it was that it pitted two of my core leadership principles against each other. In the same way that as a leader we may often be faced with the competing needs of the task and our people, our principles of leadership may come under similar pressure.

It is partly for this reason that leadership is often described as a lonely job and it is also for this reason that we must base our leadership philosophy on an understanding of what it means to be a leader.

In that moment, part of me really wanted to speak my truth and to act with integrity. On the other hand I was thinking of the soldiers for whom I was responsible. Would speaking my truth really help them and was that the best course of action for me to be of service to them?

And of course I would be lying if I did not admit to thoughts of what my last year in the army could have been like if I had really spoken my truth—telling your commanding officer that you have an issue with his words, actions and potentially his leadership style is not the done thing in the army.

I still regret it though.

Regrets cannot change what actually happened, however when we act in ways that, in hindsight, seem to be failures, we are on the path to mastery. For mastery is not achieved by making all the right choices and knowing exactly how to act in every situation—mastery is about honing one's craft and learning from our mistakes.

I have enjoyed an amazing career, received some world-class training and worked for some truly inspiring leaders. I have learned a lot along the way, had some great successes and learned a great deal from these. And I have experienced some spectacular failures that I learned even greater lessons from.

As masters, we use those regrets to ensure we make different choices and act in contrasting ways for the future. In doing so, we appreciate the value in every experience, use the emotion of regret to be better and discover the secrets of being a leader, rather than doing leadership.

One of the most powerful ways that we can move towards mastery as a leader is often the most uncomfortable for many of us; by inviting others to offer feedback. Some of us are much more comfortable seeking and receiving feedback than others, be that in connection with what we do well or what we could do differently.

My natural tendency puts me into the camp of people for whom receiving feedback does not come naturally, I have to work at it. I used to be equally bad at accepting praise as I am at accepting developmental feedback.

Early in my corporate career I recall a time when all of the senior leadership team undertook a personality profiling exercise. It was a fairly typical process. Complete an online form and attend a day-long workshop where we all received a lengthy report describing how we communicate on a good day and a bad day.

As soon as I began reading my report I was surprised at how accurate much of it was. During the workshop, our facilitator then asked us to highlight any parts of the report that we didn't think reflected us accurately and then to go and show the report to the person that knows us the most.

That evening I handed my report to Jo without any explanation of the highlighted sections.

"Why have you highlighted these bits?" Jo asked ten minutes later.

When I told her they were the areas I did not believe were accurate, she immediately replied, "Are you kidding? That's totally you!"

We all have aspects of our character that are unknown to us, often described as our blind spots. These blind spots are often a strength that begins to work against us when overplayed.

Regardless of their source, we can usually only identify them by asking others for feedback and listening to what they say. It can feel difficult and uncomfortable, though it brings two major advantages.

We improve as leaders; we are clearer on the things we could do better at, plus we build and develop huge levels of trust in our teams. The mere act of being a little vulnerable with those that we lead says a lot about our strength of character, it models the way for others to follow and it sends a clear message that we are serious about mastering leadership.

Following that exercise, I shared my full profile with my HR team, which had a significant impact on how we communicated and worked together. I have a naturally analytical brain, so when I am under pressure, my natural response is to quietly analyse the problem and work through a solution by myself.

This is often perceived by others, especially those with a different communication style to my own as being aloof, arrogant or disinterested. Reading this in my report hit me really hard and it has been something that I have been acutely aware of ever since.

Those three characteristics are so far from how I believe myself to operate that the thought of others perceiving me in that way was profound.

When I showed my team that report their response was one of amazement, with one team member saying, "This makes so much sense now. There have been times when we really thought that we'd p****ed you off Ben, but it turns out you were just thinking."

It is funny to think that so many problems within teams and communication challenges are matters of simple misunderstandings or different styles of behaving.

This was an easy change for me to make as a leader seeking mastery, yet it was one that has had a big impact. These insights only come when we are prepared to step out of our comfort zone and be a little vulnerable.

As my eyes adjusted to the shroud around me, I could now see Dr Know clearly through the gloom. He was tall and somewhat handsome, yet those piercing eyes gave a somewhat alien quality. His henchman still looked like a minotaur.

"I am hosting a comedy gala in two days' time!" Dr Know announced with a tone that could be misconstrued as pleasure. "All my so-called evil genius compatriots will be in attendance—I'll say one thing for sociopathic tyrants, they do have a remarkable sense for the humorous!"

"Why are you telling me this?" I finally broke my silence, more from a state of confusion than a willingness to go along with whatever scheme Dr Know was hatching.

"All I have ever done is seek to better myself. That single pursuit has forced me to make some infeasibly tough decisions that some misinterpret as villainy." He paused for a moment; perhaps in sadness or regret, but perhaps not. "Those monsters do not seek to better anything—they simply desire the power to take, to destroy, to stop the pain they feel by inflicting it upon other people!"

"The challenge with despotic leaders is that they always see themselves as justified in their actions." I murmured.

"It is the line we all walk, Mr Morton!" Dr Know smiled. "If you want to capture your enemies, they will all be there… unsuspecting and unprepared."

"Where is this gala being held?" I asked, taking the bait. Dr Know intensified his already intimidating glower.

"Oh, I am sure you'll find me, Mr Morton… you are very good at punishing yourself!" He cackled in a strangely maniacal way that caught me off guard. Distracted for merely the briefest of moments, Dr Know and his sidekick slithered into the darkness and were gone.

I leapt forward to stop their escape, but there was no sign of either man. I turned back towards the tunnel and peered out into the darkness, but could see no movement. Somewhat bemused I started along the passage and up towards street level, where my team would be waiting.

Mission: Reconnaissance and Retrieval

1. As a leader, to what degree do you speak your truth, where 1 is never and 10 is all of the time without question? (Note: 10 is not necessarily the ideal score)

2. To what degree do you reflect upon and learn from your successes and your failures: where 1 is never and 10 is I have the discipline and a robust personal system for doing it?

3. How good are you at seeking feedback, be that from your team, peers, customers, suppliers, etc.?

What impact is all of the above having on your ability to lead?

The Man with the Olden Pun

"What did he mean by punishing myself?" I asked, staring at my loyal team of four agents. "I mean, I have had my fair share of black eyes and cracked ribs, and sure I've been tortured on numerous occasions, but punishing myself?"

"Maybe," Agent M pondered. "It is not punishing as in punishment, but to be *punish*, as in a joke?"

I glanced at Agent V, who turned to her computer terminal and said, "I'm on it!"

After a hurried succession of keystrokes, Agent V brought up a list of the ten most corny comedians in Britain. Top of the list was a man whose jokes were so old and unfunny that he was known as *The Man with the Olden Pun*.

"That's not all," Agent V explained, peering intently at the screen. "He's appearing in two days' time at a comedy gala on the cruise ship *Supremacy*. The ship is sailing in the morning from Southampton!"

I regarded my team with a sense of gratitude and genuine affection. "Well, it seems as though we are going on holiday!"

Mission: Leadership

When I left the army I went from directly leading a team of around six and being the second in command for a squadron of around 180 soldiers, to World Challenge where I was leading a team of two others, with a third team member for four months of the year.

The way my team was structured back then meant that I was involved in a lot of the doing of things. I was running training events and selection courses for our seasonal expedition leaders, plus I was spending a lot of time recruiting people to lead expeditions for us.

It was doing the doing that allowed me to not only prove my capability, but to also build a business case for expanding the team. Whilst I knew that I personally had a lot of doing to do, I was also aware that I needed to step back; to lead and think strategically about the role.

When I took over responsibility for the team at World Challenge it felt as if I were being handed a poisoned chalice. I was constantly reminded by virtually everybody in the company, how none of my predecessors had lasted more than one or two years in the role.

Those who had undertaken the role before me thought they could solve the leader recruitment problem yet no one did. Recruiting was viewed as attempting to fill with water a bucket that had holes shot into it. When I regarded the person I was taking over from (and the team that was staying), my overarching observation was that they were tired, really tired.

What enabled me to break that cycle in which we were trapped was a series of leadership philosophies. At that time, they were deep within me and existed as unconscious traits I had gleaned over my lifetime, instead of a fully-functional ethos. Putting these traits to work in real-world scenarios has enabled me to develop them into ten discrete principles; principles I will be sharing with you later.

I can be extremely determined, even dogged—when someone says to me that something cannot be done or will not work. I have, what at times can be an unreasonably strong desire to prove them wrong! This also contributed to the turnaround in recruitment at World Challenge.

As the massive liner, Supremacy, headed out into the open ocean the atmosphere among our team was pensive and rather subdued. We could not even begin to know what lay ahead for us on this trip. Was this indeed a comedy gala for the rich, powerful and very deranged? Or was this a trap set for us by the manipulative Dr Know?

As we sat around our cabin, each of us was lost in our own thoughts. The weight of my own introspection was almost too heavy a burden; we were here to carry out our mission, yet my rogue status put every member of my team in jeopardy. The needs of the task we faced seemed to pale in comparison to what would happen to my team if we continued on this path.

I needed some time to step back; a moment of pause to assess my strategy and decide the best course of action. So, with my tuxedo looking sharp and hair perfectly styled, I did what all good spies do—I visited the bar for a Martini.

People and leaders are busy.

This is an accepted aspect of modern working life. When asked how they are in a work context, most people will reply, "busy" or "really busy". Some say this because they feel they should (anything other than being busy would suggest they are not good at what they do, or they are not an effective leader).

We are all busy, work is busy, the world is busy—technology makes it even busier and we find it harder to disconnect. The challenge is that much of the time, we can be busy fools.

Most are under great pressure—we have a lot to get done in the space of a working day. At the same time we know there are inefficiencies and problems in the way that we are working; we just tell ourselves that we do not have time to stop and think. So we stay on this downward spiral of busy-ness.

When a person is successful in their professional role they will often be promoted to a position of greater responsibility and one that essentially requires them to go meta to their original job. Upon promotion they work harder, faster and longer.

Rather than leading others in the successful completion of the tasks at hand, they do what they have always done, repeating the same work, never letting go, refusing to delegate. In this way they do not become a leader; they become a super-manager.

A super-manager does not inspire others to act and they do not build great teams and organisations in the long term. We therefore have a choice to make, we can either work smarter or work harder. This is only the illusion of a choice however, because only one path has a viable outcome. You can take the path of leadership towards long-term success by working smarter, or take the route to super-manager, short-term success and eventual burnout.

The leader's imperative is to focus on leading; even when we are busy doing the doing, we must make time for leading, for stepping back, for creating the headspace to think. Contrast this to the super-manager who leads in their spare time.

Taking a long-term view shifts our attention from the alluring distraction of the immediate. This requires confidence. It takes nerve to say no to short-term rewards for the sake of results that are further away. Nonetheless, this is the essence of leadership—looking to the future and creating a long-term plan; a vision to strive for.

When I looked at that exhausted team; these burned out people that I was now responsible for at World Challenge, I was conscious of a number of things...

The success of my team, and to a degree the business, was going to come down to my ability to balance the needs of delivering the task (hitting our recruitment numbers with quality people) whilst really looking after every member of the team.

I was clear in my mind from the start that I did not want to be scrabbling around trying to recruit the last expedition leader twenty-four hours before the excited team of kids departed on their adventure of a lifetime. I was equally clear that I was not going to find myself sitting at my desk in a year's time, leading a team that were as shattered as they were in that moment. I also had no desire to feel that way myself.

It was equally apparent to me that I had a duty of care to my team. If they were in the same position in twelve months' time, I would have failed in that duty of care. If I had hit my targets and recruited all of the expedition leaders, but the team were in the same state I was clear in my mind that I would have failed as a leader.

It is not just about the task—what we do at work, how hard we work, how tired and stressed we feel and how we achieve success as leaders, all have a huge impact on every aspect of our lives, both in work and out of the workplace.

I was unable to crack the recruitment problem in that first year. We ended the year still fighting to find the last few leaders, we were tired and we had worked really hard. However, we were not nearly as tired as we could have been and we were in a better position than the year before. There was real progress, so we celebrated those small victories and learned from them.

The main contrast to the previous year is that we were ready to go again, to take a second bite of the apple. We were now working smarter and we had sown the seeds for getting better. We had a vision of where we were going, which enabled us to break the downward trend and create an upward spiral.

As my drink arrived, I noticed a familiar face across the cocktail bar... it was Meg Lomanya. Turning away to face the bar, so as not to be spotted, I continued my vigil by watching her in the mirrored tiles of the bar area.

She was talking to a tall man that I did not recognise; thankfully she was so lost in laughter and conversation that she had not seemed to notice me. After five minutes or so, another man sidled up to Lomanya and whispered in her ear. She bade farewell to her original companion and left with the messenger. I took the opportunity to follow her.

Ensuring that I would not be seen, I trailed behind my quarry as she swept down corridors and up flights of stairs. Eventually we stepped out onto on the ship's upper decks. It was only then I noticed how the liner had slowed to almost a complete halt. The reason for this was apparent in the enormous metal tripod that towered from the ocean and stood many hundreds of feet above us.

This gargantuan construction must be the oceanic headquarters of this evil axis of villains. The comedy gala was less stand up and more tear down; for looking around me, I realised I was standing amongst the most fearsome leaders of the underworld. Maniacal tyrants, hell-bent on the destruction of all I stood for.

I needed to get on board that immense base and I must do this alone—I could not risk my team any more than I had already. Before I left the ship, however, I sent one last message to my team...

Project Eye-Full

Mission: Reconnaissance and Retrieval

CLASSI

1. On a 1-10 spectrum, where 1 is super-manager and 10 is a great leader, where would you place yourself?

2. In general do you tend to think short term or long term, where 1 is we just react to the day-to-day, and 10 is we plan ahead to get on a positive, upward spiral?

3. How well do you balance the needs of the team and the task?

What impact is all of the above having on your ability to lead?

Eye-Full

Having slipped aboard the massive oceanic tripod, blending in with a large group who had obviously been invited to whatever was about to take place, I slipped away by passing through a hefty side door. This led me along a narrow corridor and past several large bulkheads.

Despite the relative quiet of this corridor, the constant creaking and groaning of the structure seemed to weave with my own breathing and heartbeat. This strangely incongruous symphony caused me some unease; how would I hear the approach of those I most certainly did not want to encounter?

This was one of those occasions when I would have benefited from villains who had a sense of customer service and actually provided some form of navigation aid. A map, schematic or even the odd sign would have served me well, but no, I would need to find my own way to wherever I was going.

The corridor turned sharply to the right, followed by a steep crew-ladder to the lower decks. I supposed I was heading down into the heart of this three-legged vessel. Before heading down the first ladder, I paused and developed a plan... What was my objective? How did that ideally look? What type of arbitrary factors might I encounter?

I constructed my vision for success, thinking quickly and effectively. Then with a deep breath I clutched the slim rails either side of the ladder; swung out into the void below and slid into the unknown.

Whilst leading the recruitment and training team at World Challenge we held a distinct vision—one that we constantly worked towards. We had a written statement of where we wanted to be and this was clearly linked to the organisation's goals.

Our vision also had an unwritten context that was hugely motivating to us all. This came from the joint understanding of our vision; what it would mean to us personally, to our colleagues, to the freelance staff we were responsible for recruiting, and for the teachers and students who went on our expeditions.

Our mission was "To be the outdoor industry's employer of choice."

On first glance it may seem a little generic. Yet, it was short, simple and easy to remember. Once a team member knew the complete picture of our working environment and how we were viewed by many in our industry at the time, they appreciated just how aspirational our vision was.

Overall, our mission was a huge ask for each of us—it supposed a reality that was far removed from our current situation. Although, whenever we had discussions around the vision, it felt very real, compelling and achievable. Each time the team started talking about our vision, we connected to it.

Realisation of our vision would make us the market leaders in our field; other businesses would be coming to us for training and the knowledge of how we did it. To be the employer of choice would negate the stress of trying to recruit expedition leaders at the last minute. And when an expedition leader did drop out at the last minute, we would have people to call on, those who were desperate to travel at the drop of a hat.

Through the attainment of our vision we could be offering such great service to the expedition leaders, looking after them so well, paying them fairly and investing in their development. The teachers and students would be immensely happy, which would also result in fewer complaints to deal with after the expeditions.

As part of a successful team, things would not be so last minute and frantic, there would be less pressure and we would feel less stressed. The dread of that crazy four weeks in the summer would dissipate. My chest pains would go... I would be less stressed at home... I would not snap so much at others...

Life would be good...

I wanted to work hard to get to that place.

In the army, the word vision was not used a great deal, if at all. However, we had our own language that served the same purpose—the purpose of ensuring that everyone knew exactly what we were striving to achieve.

Whenever I received or gave a set of orders for a particular operation or task, there would be specific pieces of information offered in a particular order. The first was my superior officer's intent (Commander's Intent—one up). This was followed by my commander's commander's intent (Commander's Intent—two up).

With this information, I always understood where my role fitted into the bigger picture—in current terminology, where it fitted into the overall vision or strategy. This made decision-making a speedier process.

When I knew why I was doing what I was doing and how that related to the bigger picture, I could react quickly if the situation changed. Instead of going back to my commander and explaining the situation had changed, I could just react, as I knew ultimately what we were working towards.

This never happened at Tesco. I never discovered what my boss's boss's intent was, and on the off-chance that I did, I had no faith in their commitment to the intent. As their actions failed to match their words so consistently, over time my trust was eroded away.

Normally, when a leader asks the question, "Why do my team come to me for the answers all of the time?" or, "Why can't they think for themselves more and come to me with possible solutions?" they themselves are part of the problem.

Is the team or individual clear what they are working towards? Are they clear on the overall vision, the bigger picture, the strategy or what the leader is working towards? Has the leader communicated the mission clearly and with adequate context?

Another element that was crucial when I was issuing and receiving orders in the military was the language used. For each mission we were about to complete, each word was specifically chosen—they needed to be unambiguous and to give an absolutely clear picture of what must be done.

In war movies, characters will often utter phrases such as *take out*.

I remember hearing one of my colleagues at Sandhurst using those words during a training exercise; the feedback from our instructor was rather apt...

"I'm going to take out my wife at the weekend. We don't take out enemy positions. We destroy enemy positions."

There was no doubt about the clarity of what we were doing. This is a blessing when you consider that in southern Iraq I went on to capture known insurgents and secure and defend the key strategic port of Umm Qasr. The taking out of any of these factors could have been embarrassing!

Various sets of ladders and corridors led me to a kitchen area, where several tuxedoed waiters gathered trays of drinks to distribute amongst the guests. For a change, my own attire would help me to go unnoticed, rather than causing me to stand out, as was usually the case!

Discreetly, I collected a tray and filled it with flutes of champagne; this way I was able to blend in with the servers around me. Thankfully, nobody seemed to notice the interloper amongst them. With the tray full, I followed the steady stream of waiters through the service doors of the galley and out into a vast ballroom.

Considering the location of this hall, situated within a large metallic tripod in the middle of the ocean, it was exquisite in its grandeur and elegance. From lavish chandeliers to fine artwork, long, luxurious drapes and furniture of fine oak. The hall was crowded with people dressed in the best finery; many of whom I had encountered before on my missions.

It was time to set my trap, ensure that all was in place and then get out of there as quickly as possible. This three-legged construction now housed the world's most dangerous villains and their associates. In one swift move I could capture the enemy and secure this strategic position. It was time to commence *Project Eye-Full*; a covert programme specially designed for this very scenario.

After a brief reconnoitre of the area, checking entrances and exits, I made my way back out to the corridor and removed my phone from my jacket. With a few taps of my fingers, I composed a message for my team.

> Eye-Full Go.

Almost instantly the reply came back...

> Get out of there, Ben, it's a trap!

It is often said that the first ninety days in a new role are critical. Convention encourages you to ask all the stupid questions in the first few months as you will look foolish after that. Another common piece of erroneous advice is to really make the most of your induction period as there will never be the time to go back and discover what people do after that.

For me, both of these display grave errors in judgement.

When I began my new job at World Challenge, I thought back to my experiences as an aspiring, trainee army officer. The advice I was given was equally as valuable when I applied it to my transition from the army into the corporate world as a leader.

Just as I was encouraged to put on a pair of coveralls in the army and change the oil on a truck with other soldiers, I took the same philosophy forward with me in every job. Getting under the truck was partly to understand what my soldiers did, partly getting to know them. Both are hugely valuable to leaders.

Now, this may be easier when you are starting a new role as it is expected to a certain degree. The same principle can still apply when you have been leading the same team, department or business for months, even years.

It can become marginally trickier the more senior you are, in terms of your actual leadership position within an organisation, although this is not always the case. In many instances that particular ethos is caused by the worry of what others will think, rather than the reality of the circumstances.

Some of the most profound moments of growth for me as a leader, outside the army, came from getting stuck in and doing the doing for a while. In all these instances I either needed to due to the circumstance or I chose to in order to grow. I have always had a degree of intentionality about this and I encourage you to do the same.

At World Challenge I observed the leader selection training courses for a while and then jumped into the facilitation of those same courses—this was a big part of my job.

Soon after I took over the head of HR role, my recruitment officer resigned so I had to return to recruitment for several months whilst I found a replacement.

What, on the surface, seemed like a problem was actually a great opportunity. It presented me with a massive insight into what we did well, what we did badly and where we could improve.

When the new recruitment officer arrived, I shared my observations, gave her time to make her own judgements and then gave her the freedom to get on and make things better.

Similarly, when I started at Tesco, I observed some of the leadership courses being run which gave me insights into what worked and what did not. When I moved into the Tesco Online Academy there was much physical work to be done on the site itself, so I invested a lot of time exploring this, as it gave me great insights into the process going forward.

Everything I learnt from my career in the army and the challenges of my roles in the corporate world helped me to create a vision for my own future—one where I stepped out of my comfort zone and into the world of self-employment.

At Tesco I was doing a job that did not play to my strengths. For much of my working day I was so caught up in the corporate struggle—the desire to move up and trying to prove my value—I failed to notice how unsuitable the role was.

There was no indication that the leadership principles and values that had become such a part of my being were valued or appreciated at Tesco. The situation had become so dire that upon evaluating the state of my career, even I had forgotten the things I held so close to me for so long.

I felt undervalued, restrained and restricted. I was not able to make decisions or take any action. Everything needed to be signed off by my manager, have a discussion paper written and then be approved by my boss's boss or a committee. It was stifling and claustrophobic, going against the principles of Mission Command.

Not only was I unclear on what the team was meant to be achieving, our vision and mission—I had no freedom to act with autonomy. My manager or his manager really knew very little about me or my capabilities. This was indicative of the command and control, low trust culture. And it was killing me.

Two weeks after the events on Dr Know's secret oceanic base, Ms L sat alone in her office, smiling at her visual display screens. Upon these, Dr Know stared back, his expression mysterious, yet with a hint of sinister glee.

"Congratulations," he said, his voice slightly metallic and thin through the computer's speaker. "You have wiped out every known villain in the Western world and terminated your most problematic agent!"

"I could not have done it without your help, Dr Know!" Her wry grin caused her lips to tighten as she spoke.

"And I shall hold you to that debt!" He almost broke a smile. "Though I too benefit from you wiping out my competition!"

"Now you have the monopoly on underworld goings-on, the assurance of my cooperation and..." she paused. "Agents that do as they're told and will not interfere in our business!"

"Our business?" He asked, knowingly.

"Of course! You didn't think I was going to let you have all the fun, did you?" Ms L giggled with a manner that seemed far too frivolous for her demeanour.

"And what of Morton's team? I do hope they will not be... problematic?" There was an edge to his tone.

"As far as they are concerned, they were duped into following a rogue agent," she explained, her voice permeated with a mix of cunning and pride. "They are utterly grateful for my compassionate leniency and willingness to look past the treasonous crimes... you do not have to worry about them!"

"Well, until we meet again!" Dr Know raised a glass of wine into view. Ms L matched his gesture with a Scotch.

"Until next time!" She exclaimed cheerfully.

The window that had been framing Dr Know's face disappeared from the screen to reveal the profile of a covert agent—the word *Deceased* stamped across the page. Behind this was a news article detailing the destruction of the world's super-villains in a missile attack, conducted by the British military.

"Goodnight, Mr Morton. Goodnight!" She whispered, raising her glass with a broad, self-satisfied grin. "Sleep tight and don't let the fishes bite!"

Her smile disappeared suddenly as she noticed an envelope on her desk; it was addressed simply to Ms L. With urgency, she snatched the letter and ripped it open with a jagged tear across the top. Unfolding the contents, her eyes widened as she read.

Dear Ms L... Please take this letter as notice of my resignation... Kind Regards... Mr Ben Morton.

She lowered the letter gently to her lap and gazed into the darkness, over her computer screens. The glint of light reflected from a revolver's barrel had caught her attention.

"Morton?" She called hesitantly. "Morton, is that you?"

Mission: Reconnaissance and Retrieval

1. On a scale of 1-10, how clear are those in your team on the vision and the specific part they have to play in making it a reality?

2. On a scale of 1-10, how well do you share your intent with your team, thus allowing them to respond quickly and stay agile?

3. On a scale of 1-10, how much time do you spend talking with your team, customers and suppliers to understand things from their perspective?

What impact is all of the above having on your ability to lead?

Prime Target... Marcy Systyck

Section Three

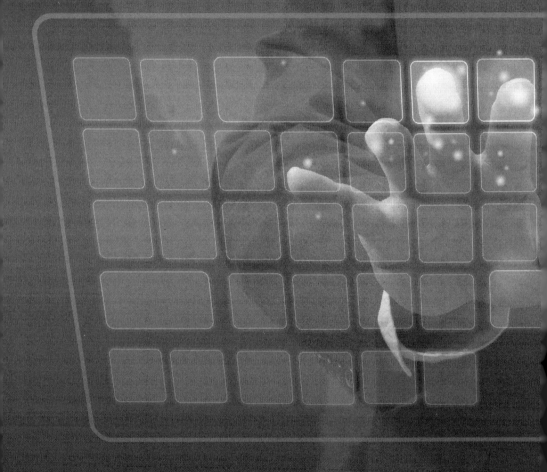

Business Leadership|

The Ten Principles of Leadership

The role of leaders in business is changing. Technological evolution is increasingly rapid, the leaders of tomorrow need to operate by fundamentally different means. These will require different skills and behaviours that are congruent with a world that no longer conforms to the conventions we have all grown up with.

These changes not only shift the way we use language, but also the way we socialise, our lifestyle behaviour and our global culture. Twenty years ago, our main form of written communication was by letter and people formed relationships socially; now we emoji a quick WhatsApp message and couples decide to get married on the basis of Facebook communication!

For many companies, and various industries, the very nature of work is changing too. The ever-shifting sands have huge implications for how we manage, lead and look after those who work for us.

Much of the management theory that is currently applied within our workplaces today has its origins in the industrial revolution. A time when management involved sweating our assets, both mechanical and human—this implied getting the maximum productivity from people who largely worked on production lines.

Many of those in leadership positions are managing knowledge workers with Industrial-Revolution-based thinking—all the while, scratching their heads and wondering why their people are not better engaged!

When a leader takes the approach of old-style leading, in an area of their own expertise, micromanaging will often ensue. In extreme cases, the manager will develop super-manager tendencies which may have limited success in the immediate or short term, but in the long run will fail, as the manager attempts to do everything themselves.

Micromanagement goes against my own fundamental truth about leadership. I have experienced first-hand the effects of micromanagement—I know how that made me feel and it was not a feeling I ever want to impose on others.

When I was micromanaged I felt miserable, was disengaged and apathetic towards my work. Yet, resisting the temptation to fall into the micromanaging trap has been a constant leadership challenge for me.

I am very much a perfectionist; always striving to ensure that anything my team and I deliver is the best that it can possibly be. At the same time I am also driven by a growth mindset. No matter how well my team and I have delivered, I will still look to identify ways that could make it even better.

This approach has often led me to want to do things myself. Because I know how I want it done and I am clear what good looks like.

Hence, my natural urge can be to delegate the What and How. These very natural motivations enable me to identify with leaders in the same position—knowing those same urges and the impact they have, I appreciate how hard it can be in the reality of the daily workload.

Understanding this dichotomy between the ideal and the real world also enables me to see the value in encouraging leaders to provide the *what* and *why* and delegate the *how*. This is the military ethos of leadership based upon a Mission Command approach.

Being intentional about all aspects of leadership, understanding that although leadership is about others it starts with us, enables us to transcend the egocentric urge to micromanage and helps us step into true leadership.

One's own style of leadership is just one of the challenges a leader faces; as businesses adapt and grow to match the context of a technological age, it is those in leadership positions that find themselves furthest from their comfort zone.

Not so long ago leaders could rely on their functional expertise and experience as the basis for their leadership. It was highly likely that whatever challenge someone in their team brought to them, they would have experienced it before.

The future holds a completely different scenario—as a leader, you will be expected to help people solve challenges that you have no experience in whatsoever. Perhaps an even greater conundrum is when you find yourself trying to help team members solve a challenge that neither you nor they have experience in.

In these instances, a powerful and effective way forward is to coach your team. With expert questioning and exploration both individually and as a team, you can tease out the answers and solutions that have, so far, evaded detection. Through regular and consistent coaching, teams can venture into this new, unknown landscape with confidence, adaptability and the knowledge that whatever comes, they can handle it.

The way you communicate with your team, empowering them with a Mission Command approach to achieving the desired outcome, and coaching them through times when the expertise is beyond the current knowledge are important aspects of modern leadership. However, there is one consideration that is an absolute must for any leader who is going to succeed in our evolving world.

As technology becomes more advanced, affecting every aspect of our lives from social and business communications, to professional, business and even cultural dynamics, each of us is monitored more closely. The old notions of personal privacy are gradually eroding and so much of what we think, say and do is exposed for others to find.

The disparity between who you genuinely are, and who you present yourself as to the world, now impacts us personally, professionally and it is intrinsically tied to our business. This increasing transparency comes with a need for absolute authenticity. If you simply do the model, people will see right through you and know that you are being disingenuous.

The leaders of our radically changing world need to approach models in a fundamentally different way; to determine how a model aligns with one's own personal values, allow that model to create deep and lasting change within, and then place the model to one side, allowing the underlying change to produce authentic leadership behaviour.

Models are a method of communication, nothing more. And just as communication in other forms is changing, so must the way we use models. Modelling the symptomatic behaviour of an expert, reducing those behaviours into bite-sized chunks and mimicking them step by step is now perceived as charlatanism.

Models can still be of use when the way we approach them is adapted to one where we interact with the deeper experience behind those models. But for every leader, the real need for change comes with us living and breathing the principles of leadership.

On this journey so far, you have seen how my own military leadership enabled me to prepare for, and on two occasions, go to war. After five years of active service, I used my skills as an officer in the British Army to find some success, and various failures, in the corporate world of covert leadership. Here, the application of army leadership cannot simply be transferred to the business context; it needs adapting and refining for the different environment.

As a business owner and self-employed coach, I have been able to refine ways of taking covert leadership and making it a transformational, absolutely authentic methodology for becoming an inspiring business leader. Here the models of undercover missions and secret objectives are left behind, in favour of a series of principles that will help you become the best leader you can be.

These ten principles of leadership come into their own when approached in conjunction with your own values and beliefs. Rather than doing the checklist, where the steps of each model are ticked off one by one, here you are invited to make the principles your own; finding your own approach to being a true leader along the way.

I believe these leadership principles are so powerful because they are not models that you apply—these foundations can be aligned with your own core values to form a transformative force.

This force is like electricity or gravity—understanding the principles is like understanding gravity. Gravity does what it does whether you believe in it or not. However, when you understand how gravity works, you can operate more effectively in the world.

For instance, if you model a champion cyclist to understand how they became a champion, you may focus on when they train, how long for and what they eat, etc. These factors will certainly contribute to their success, but there are so many underlying aspects to their winning approach that simply doing what they do will not be as effective for you.

Your body may need different foods to achieve the same results, you may need to train harder, faster, or pull the intensity right back to a routine that suits you. Even if you get down to what they are thinking before, during and generally around times of intense training, it is often what they are unaware of in their training perspective that makes all the difference.

Modelling has so many holes and knowledge gaps that it can only ever communicate a partial illustration of what you need to do. Furthermore, if you just do the model, you are failing to appreciate a fundamental truth... The champion who was modelled is not doing a model—they are being a champion!

The following principles are a way to evoke the spirit of leadership. Armed with these ten essential criteria for being a successful leader, you can align yourself with the very infrastructure of great leadership. You can focus on who you are, what your values stand for and how you see yourself in the world. With your heart and mind aligned, you can then let the powerful forces of real leadership flow from you and inspire your team.

In other words, these leadership principles are the *what* and the *why*, not the *how*... You can observe how others do great leadership, but only you can know how you can be a great leader!

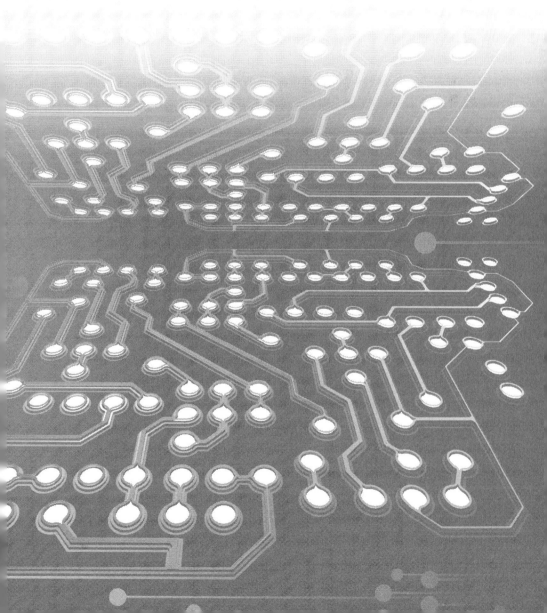

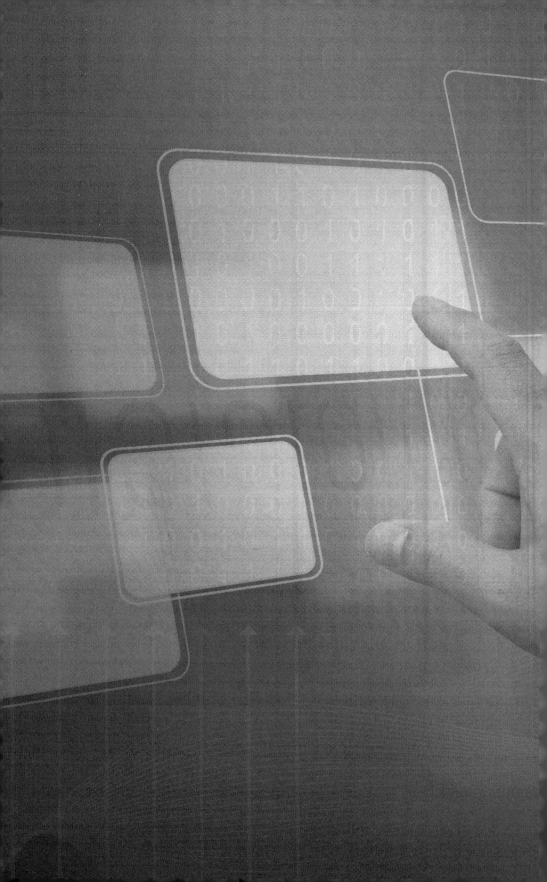

Principle One—
Serve to lead

- The primary role of a leader is to provide leadership, not be doing the doing.
- We must put the needs of those that we lead ahead of our own.
- This principle helps us to know when to lead from the front and when to lead from behind. Asking ourselves which we should do in order to be of most service to the individuals, to the team and to the organisation.

As leaders we are rewarded for providing leadership, which is often confused with working harder and longer. The latter approach is not leadership—it is becoming a super-manager.

This is merely a short-term strategy. It is also a strategy that often leads to burnout, health problems and a wake of broken relationships, be they family or colleagues.

When we accept the higher pay cheque, we accept the privilege and responsibility of leadership. We are committing to the care of those in our charge, putting their needs ahead of own.

Steve Radcliffe suggests in his book, *Leadership: Plain and Simple*, "In leader mode, your first thought is not 'what shall I do?' It's 'who do I want to engage and what is the request I want to make of them?'" This is an important consideration throughout your leadership journey, although the more senior you are in an organisation, the more significant it becomes.

To truly appreciate the value of this ethos, let us examine the Leadership Equaliser:

1. As the leader of a team, consisting of a few people, you will be doing a large amount of doing things, a fair level of managing things and very little time actually leading.

2. In a mid- to senior-management role, you need to be doing less, considerably more managing and a significant degree of leading

3. As a director, MD, CEO or divisional head, you must be minimising the doing of tasks, little to some managing and investing the great majority of your time in leading.

A friend and colleague of mine, Brian Lumsdon, once shared his take on Leadership with a capital *L*, when compared with leadership, small *l*.

Leadership can come about when you have an official title that reflects your leader status. When you are the head of a team, department, business and so on— this is the essence of capital *L*, Leadership. The small *l* version of leadership can be achieved by anybody and everybody, regardless of title.

By defining leadership as the act of serving others, of inspiring them and presenting a tangible sense of what they can achieve in the future, then we do not need a title to be a leader. Through our words and actions, each of us lead others in every situation and various contexts.

As leaders, if we do not have time for our people or enough time to think ahead to the long term, then chances are that we are busy doing the wrong things. In these instances, we have failed to adjust the dials on the Leadership Equaliser as we have taken on more demanding or more senior leadership roles.

Another reason for our lack of time may be that we have slipped back into doing what we have always done before. For a while, we may have adjusted the dials on our equaliser, but an influx of work has forced us back into old habits.

It is important to note that they are old habits and not necessarily bad habits. The ways of working that we once employed as a team leader or manager will have served us well then. Although what got you there will not necessarily get you where you are going next.

One way to make more time for leading may be to look at all of the activities that you can stop doing altogether or the roles you can delegate. As leaders it can be hard to let go of the aspects of our work that we enjoy doing. These may be things that we are good at, systems or processes that we created previously, or it may even be a client relationship that we nurtured over many years.

The crux of the issue is to be really honest with yourself and to ask whether you are really the one who should be doing those activities.

There may also be aspects of your work that you, and your team, continue to do because you always have, even if these are adding no value at all. The best leaders seek out these time-vacuums with an eye to eliminating them—they achieve this by continually asking why. Why are we doing this? Why do we have to do this? Why is it done this way? Why can't we just stop doing it?

Freek Vermeulen (Associate Professor of Strategy and Entrepreneurship at London Business School), described how in 2004 the Independent Newspaper was under financial pressure and facing an uncertain future.

The paper began to investigate ways of reducing costs and increasing profits, when the idea of a size-reduction for the broadsheet newspaper was suggested. This would help, because broadsheets are actually more expensive to produce than the smaller papers.

When the idea was broached, many people replied with the expected response of, "Our customers wouldn't want a smaller broadsheet, we can't do that!"

On the contrary—how often have you seen someone struggling to read a broadsheet on a busy train or aeroplane? Broadsheet papers actually came into being in 1716 when the government of the day introduced a tax on the number of pages in a newspaper. As a tax-saving measure the papers increased the size of the pages and decreased the number of pages. This law was abolished in 1835, yet the papers continued refusing to shrink the papers, simply because they did not stop to ask why.

Once you have asked why and you are sure that this activity is essential, then the next question to ask is, can you delegate this to someone in the team? If the answer is affirmative, there are some other key questions to ask...

- Who has the time to take this on?
- Who has the capability and skills to take this on?
- Who would grow and develop the most from taking this task on if I supported and coached them?

After asking yourself all of these questions you may come to the conclusion that this particular task still needs to be completed by you, which is fine. As leaders there are always tasks that we need to do ourselves—our need to do certain aspects of the job will never totally diminish.

So long as we can say with absolute honesty and integrity that we are doing this task because we have to, that is the correct decision. This is different to doing an activity because we really like that particular task or we think that it will just be easier and quicker to do it ourselves. This may be the case, but only in the short term.

As leaders we can often be of most service to our teams by stepping back and leading from behind.

This is a lesson I have kept close to my core values since early on in my military career. I maintained it throughout my corporate career and it has continued to serve me well as a leadership mentor.

Sometimes the best thing that we can do for the teams that we lead is to say nothing at all. This allows others to think and to speak before we influence them as the leader. If you are the first to offer a solution, the danger is that your people think that what you have said is your decision or your preferred solution.

This is a lesson that has been reiterated time and time again for me, during these years of working with groups, facilitating meetings or helping under-performing teams to move on.

The real skill in great leadership and effective facilitation is knowing when to remain silent, thus enabling others to speak. This is easier said than done as our ego or inbuilt desire to prove our own worth kicks in.

I have done this myself many times; when a group is discussing a thorny issue, part of me would urge me to keep quiet, let the conversation continue and see what comes out. At the same time my inner monologue would be suggesting that I jump in or worrying that I was not proving my value. All of those thoughts tend to stem from ego or our own insecurity as a leader/facilitator.

A strategic solution to this is to replace that inner monologue with a question that is more conducive to a successful outcome.

"What is the best thing for me to do or say next that will be of most service to this team?"

Often the answer will be to say nothing.

My experience of facilitating with this approach is very similar to that of leaders running meetings. The skill of a great leader is to elicit the thoughts and ideas of others first, before jumping in with their own thoughts. The greatest leaders I have worked with, and coached, are masters of combining advocacy and enquiry—if they do need to speak first to kick start the conversation, they are really clear about saying...

"...This is what I think, but I would really love to hear what you think. And let me be clear, that isn't my decision, it's just the start of the conversation."

Furthermore, when they facilitate in this style, they are also conscious of thanking those that speak next for contributing a different view; they encourage others to do the same. They have the emotional intelligence to identify those that have contributed (or perhaps are reluctant to do so, encouraging them to share their views too).

Putting the needs of those in our team ahead of our own should not be confused with doing their job for them or consistently jumping in and taking work from them when they are under pressure. It is not about prioritising their work ahead of your own—these are the behaviours of a super-manager, rather than a leader.

I must admit to falling foul of this during my own career—for all the right reasons, but with an approach that was flawed. As Head of HR at World Challenge I promoted one of my team members into my previous role.

She was hugely talented, extremely driven and more than capable, although she struggled initially with the workload. I wanted to be of service to her and the team so I jumped in and took on some of the work that I used to do.

My logic was that I would give her time to transition into the role. Upon reflection I would never take this approach again, for I suspect that my well-intentioned actions had a contradictory effect on her motivation. This is certainly what I would experience if the roles were reversed—I would have felt as if I had disappointed my boss; that I had not lived up to their expectations.

A better option would be to invest more time in helping them reprioritise their work; discovering what they could delegate.

There are occasions when the right approach is to get stuck in and help your team—I am certainly not advocating never helping your team in this way.

How do you know which approach to take?

It comes back to the principle—Serve to Lead—and that simple question, a question that you can either ask yourself internally or explicitly ask your team:

"How can I be of most service to you?"

Of course, ask that question in your own words, in a way that feels honest and congruent for you.

It could be...

"How can I be of most help to you?" or it may be...

"Would you like some help reprioritising? Can I do that for you or help in some other way?"

Whatever you do and whatever you say, always remember that, as a leader, it is your job to be of service.

Remember, if we are going to be of service to those that we lead, we must also look after ourselves and understand what we need to do in order to be at our best for the teams we lead. Despite the fact that I regularly stand in front of large groups of people and audiences, I am naturally an introvert. I am productive when working by myself and after spending time with large groups of people or conducting intensive training, I need time alone to recharge. These are the traits of an introverted personality (which is often wrongly associated with shyness) that I have come to recognise within me.

Whether we tend towards introversion or extroversion, we all need other people and good relationships to thrive. As a self-employed professional, a solid network and the support of strong relationships is essential to my success. We cannot develop a profitable business that delivers real value alone; we need mutually beneficial connections with others.

Jo will sometimes notice that I seem sluggish and a little down; a cue to give me the nudge to get together with my colleagues from TwentyOne Leadership. When there are times that we have not had much contact, I need the interaction of my extended community not only to build momentum, to energise myself for the road ahead, but also to nurture the relationship itself.

I need a team of sorts; relationships that are strong enough for me to be comfortable in making big requests. These relationships with friends, other consultants, suppliers, my virtual team and the support group of potential clients, need the investment of time and genuine effort to be real.

Just as I used to build relationships with my troops and then with the teams I led in the corporate world, I made a conscious effort to build and nurture my network in a focused way. This was not in a mercenary—what's-in-it-for-me—style of networking, but the genuine growing of strong, cooperative relationships, done with volition.

I consciously analysed my network; where relationships empowered both parties and where they weaken us. Where did I have gaps? Who did I want to be connected with? What sorts of people did I need in my network and who could I help by offering my skills? Who could help me strengthen a relationship and where did I just need to strengthen it by myself?

Even though I work for myself and by myself, I am never alone—my team is different, wider and more diverse in their relationships to me, but my network is still a team and I am still a leader. By intentionally living by my leadership principles, with focused and thoughtful effort I can still be of service to the team around me. And, whilst I am not necessarily the leader of this new team, I still provide leadership.

By serving my network through the connections we establish and relationships we grow, I left behind the view of networking so many people use— that of quickly assessing who is of most use and ditching anybody who isn't a potential sale. Instead, my networking is about how we can grow as professionals, business owners and friends, through our relationships.

Chapter Summary

1. Leaders put the needs of their team ahead of their own.

2. We are all leaders, regardless of our job title.

3. To make the transition from super-manager to leader we have to let go of some of the things that we have done in the past.

4. A leader's job is to lead; it is not to be doing the doing.

5. It is a leader's job to continually ask, "Why?" and challenge the status quo.

6. Sometimes we must lead from behind, giving our team the space and time to think, allowing them to grow and develop.

7. Leaders combine advocacy and enquiry.

8. Serving to lead is about supporting others, and is not to be confused with doing their job for them.

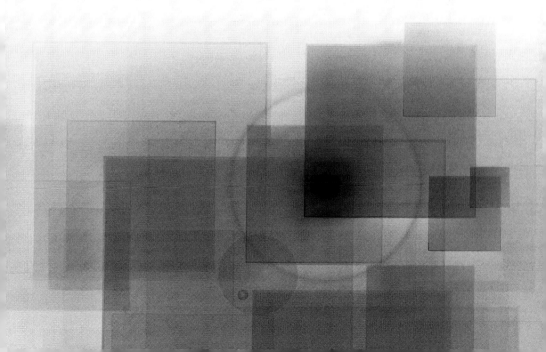

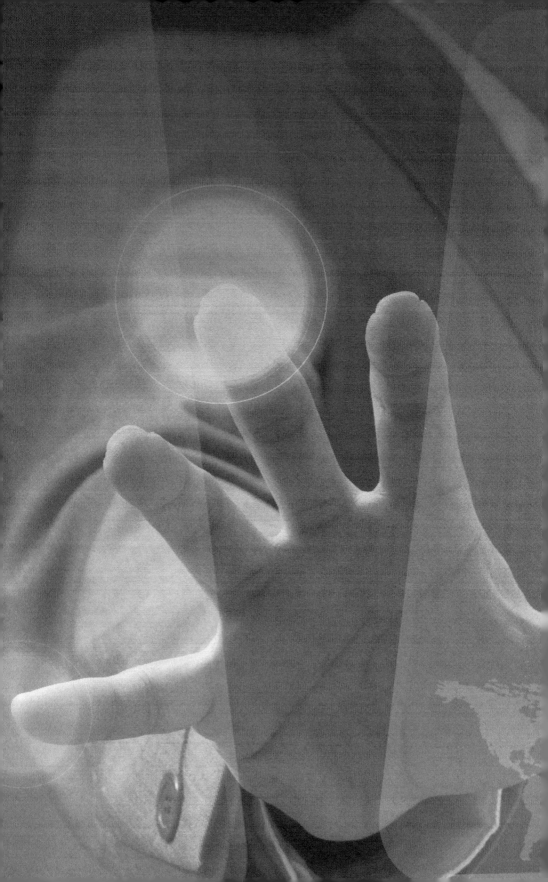

Principle Two—
You are always a leader

- Leadership is not a nine-to-five position nor is it something we do in our spare time when our other tasks are complete. Leading is our task.

- We must lead by example and be true to what we stand for. This applies whether we are in the office or at events, in person or online, through what we say, what we write and what we do.

Around the time I started my own business, I also faced my biggest ever leadership challenge—one that was more profound than anything I had previously faced in the military or corporate world.

It was a challenge which brought immense excitement and a deep sense of responsibility. If ever my belief that to lead is both a responsibility and a great privilege was to be tested, this particular leadership challenge would prove that to be true.

This ultimate test of my leadership abilities began just after lunchtime on the 9th February 2012, when my daughter Freya was born. I have come to realise that the greatest leadership challenge is the one that comes with being a parent—and it is a challenge where we will never really know how we have done.

In *Good to Great*, Jim Collins discusses Level Five leadership, which involves setting others up for success after you have gone. Being a parent is also the ultimate Level Five test. We never truly know how successful our children become.

Why am I mentioning parenthood in the context of leadership?

Parenthood is a perfect analogy for the fact that in business or in life, we are always a leader. Leadership is not something that we do between the hours of nine and five, Monday to Friday—leadership is who we are, how we behave and what we believe. If we are being leaders, instead of doing leadership, then this should not change when we leave the office to go home.

As parents we strive to set a good example for our children to follow; aspiring to do our best in developing them so that they may reach their full potential. We set out to care for them and protect them at all costs. We would gladly sacrifice our needs for our children—because that is what parents do.

That is also what great leaders do.

We would not adopt a parenting strategy where we set a good example for our children to follow, ensuring that our actions match our words, only on the odd occasion. We would not do our best for them from Saturday through to Thursday, but on Friday we let anything go because we are tired and cannot be bothered.

The same is true of leadership—in accepting the privilege and responsibility of leadership we are signing up to be a leader all of the time.

In some ways the role of a leader can feel a little unfair at times. Chances are that as leaders we will get little feedback about all of the times that we get it right. Those that we lead may not consciously notice how our actions have matched our words 99 times out of 100. They may not connect the dots and realise that we are working hard at being consistent and honest.

Those that we lead will however notice the single instance, 1 out of 100, when our actions did not match up with our words. They will notice the one time we did something that we know we should not have. They will notice the only occasion when we make a promise and fail to keep it for reasons that ought to be within our control.

As leaders, we are always leaders and our people expect us to be so.

Many people, whether in a leadership role or not, do not reveal their true selves at work. We often hear the term work-mask which describes the image that we portray at work.

The reason for wearing these masks is often based in fear—if we are insecure we may hide behind a mask of name dropping, the insecure manager may put on the mask and persona of a bully.

One of the biggest reasons for us putting on a work-mask is Imposter Syndrome.

This is a fear that most of us have experienced at some stage in our career. Here we feel that we are not up to the job, we have bitten off more than we can chew and are about to be found out. Our brains run wild creating a strong visual and emotional image of how this will unravel and what we will lose.

The associated fear with Imposter Syndrome is that we are not good enough. The idea of dropping the mask to reveal our true self fills us with dread as we imagine people looking at us and thinking, "Oh, that's who you really are!"

In terms of leadership, the person we really are is the best person we can ever be. The leadership principles that I share with you in this book are designed to make you the very best, most authentic version of you.

Oscar Wilde famously once said, "Be yourself; everyone else is taken."

And my favourite quote of all time, from Field Marshall the Viscount Slim in an address to officer cadets at Sandhurst;

"Leadership is the simplest thing in the world, because it's just plain you."

If I could be so bold as to stand on the shoulders of those who have influenced me I would perhaps add "...It's just the very best, most authentic version of you."

Putting on a work-mask has never been a good strategy for leaders. When we do so, those that we lead never truly know who we are and what we stand for. We do not seem congruent.

In the age of social media and super-connectedness, being congruent and always being a leader becomes even more important. The boundaries between work and home are less clear and less defined.

With so many social media channels at our fingertips, those that we lead, in any sense of the word, see much more of who we are and what we do. If we put on a work-mask that is very different to our natural self, those we lead will not fully trust us.

We cannot behave in one way at work and then behave in a polar-opposite fashion out of work. This is not about being a saint—it is about not pretending to be something that you are not or not hiding who you really are.

We never know when we are being recorded in some way—a single, poorly chosen tweet, Facebook update, Instagram message, blog post or even what we assume to be a private remark can undermine our authenticity.

Even if you do not have any social media accounts yourself you will be discoverable. You will appear in other people's posts, in photos or comments and you never know who is connected to them.

As leaders our duty of care to our team does not end with the working day either. I am a big advocate of maintaining a healthy work-life balance as I understand the productivity benefits that this brings. I also understand that it is critical for us as leaders to be at our best.

As a result I try to keep work and family/personal time separate; it is one of my core values. I also believe however, that the concept of working five days a week, nine-to-five is outdated.

I aim to protect my weekends from work and I strive to disconnect whilst away on holiday. What is more important, is to clearly define work and family time. If I need to work at the weekends or during holidays, I will set a period of time to do it and pull myself away from my family.

A contrast to this is when a person attempts to multitask, which results in never being fully present with those around you. I would be insufferable if I were always to get the balance right, but I try my hardest not to work when I'm spending time with my wife and daughter. I cannot bear the notion that my daughter's memories of me could be, "Dad was great, but he was always on his work phone and laptop when I was growing up."

Why do I share this? Maintaining a healthy relationship between our work and our out-of-work life is key, but we remain leaders at all times. We do not and must never stop caring about our team, merely because we have left the office or are on holiday.

In previous roles, when a member of my team has been off sick, I made it my duty and priority to check that they were okay. Did they need any support and was there anything that I or the organisation could help with? This is a leader's job; one that we should never consign to Human Resources.

Similarly, if a member of my team is working on a big presentation or project whilst I am away on leave or business, I will ensure that they know that they can contact me for support.

If it is a really big project that may require extra support, I will take the call on my holiday—and if I really am unable to (or absolutely need to disconnect so that I return refreshed and ready to serve), there are a number of actions I take before I leave.

I dedicate time to them, ensuring they have all that they need from me before I go. I will also ensure somebody else can support them in my absence and that they both know this is the plan.

Great leaders are those who step up when they are off duty or will immediately cancel personal plans when a genuine crisis hits their team or organisation. I have worked with a number of transport and service companies over the years and have been impressed by the stories that I have heard.

These are experiences of leaders stepping forward and making themselves known as an employee of the company when an issue has cropped up on a bus or a train. They did not have to—they were not wearing a uniform or name badge and none of the passengers or indeed other staff knew who they were. Yet, they stepped forward because this is what true leaders do and they understood that when we are a leader, we are always a leader.

During my early post-army career, I developed the dubious reputation of always being the last man on the dance floor. However, I was never the most inebriated, which is important. Being careful about how much alcohol I consumed meant that I could be up early the following morning.

I always looked smart and could function to the best of my ability, which demonstrated that despite being able to have fun, I was first and foremost, a leader. This was highlighted by my leaving gift—a lovely hip flask that was inscribed with the words, *Last on the dance floor, first in the office.*

This is a book about the fundamental principles of leadership and what it means to be a leader. Whilst I do not intend to provide you with a long list of tactical things to go away and do, I will venture into that arena just for a moment.

Our credibility as leaders comes from the principles and values that define us. However, it would be wrong of me to suggest that first impressions and appearances to do not have an impact upon how others view us, initially at least.

Maintaining a degree of smartness, relevant to the norms of the organisations or sector within which you work, ensuring that you are always well presented is important for us as leaders. Even when it is OK to dress more casually, such as on dress-down Fridays, I still recommend ensuring that your appearance acknowledges that you are a leader. That is not to say that you come to work wearing a suit when everyone else is in jeans, but equally I would suggest that coming to work in a tatty pair of jeans and an old t-shirt that you've just taken out of the tumble dryer isn't the approach to take either.

Your brand as a leader takes time to develop, it must be nurtured and carefully considered. The respect your team has for you can be very fragile and it can be broken a lot more quickly and easily than the time and effort it took to build. However, when you are consistent in your leadership brand, your reputation amongst your team can be utterly solid and unbreakable.

In the army we were repeatedly reminded that you cannot simply tell people to respect you and expect them to comply. Just because you are given a promotion does not automatically entitle you to respect and people will not necessarily follow you on your title alone.

We must earn trust; show our team they can follow us and our congruent actions—through our well-principled, consistent behaviour and concrete resolve to our values, we will make people want to follow us.

Chapter Summary

1. As a leader, you are always a leader.
2. Leadership is fundamentally about who you are, how you behave and what you believe.
3. Leadership is both a great privilege and a great responsibility.
4. To be a leader you must take off the work-mask and be your true, authentic self.
5. When you put on your work-mask you may appear inauthentic, inconsistent and incongruent.
6. Your duty of care to those that you lead does not finish with the end of the working day.
7. High levels of trust are at the heart of all great teams.
8. Trust and respect are earned over a period of time through a consistent and authentic approach.

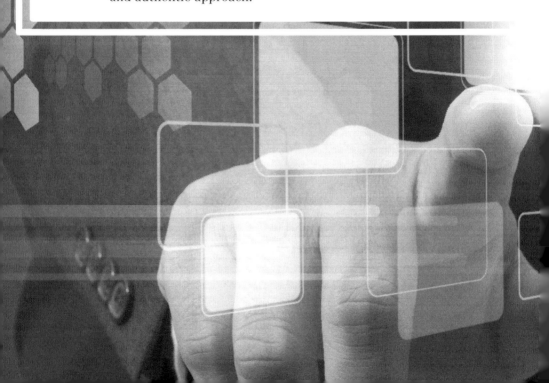

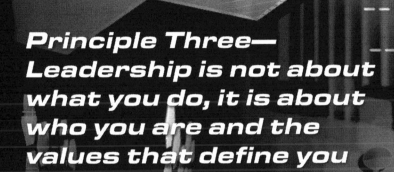

Principle Three—
Leadership is not about what you do, it is about who you are and the values that define you

- People will follow leaders for the authentic person that they are, not for the models or techniques that they apply.
- For people to know who we are, we must ourselves know what we stand for.
- Our values form our foundations—they must be our moral compass and the backstop for our decision making.

As I approached what was to be the end of my tenure at Tesco, the degree of disconnect between my values and how I was functioning in the workplace became too extreme. There was such incongruity between the Tesco experience and what I wanted to achieve with my life that I had to make a change.

These feelings eventually led me to resign, not just to find another job, but to work for myself so that I could never be made to feel like that again. Without that catalyst and experience, I would perhaps never have made the leap to running my own business.

I am by nature, risk averse—a cautious person in many respects—so setting up my own business was a huge challenge for me. Surprisingly, I have loved nearly every minute of it! My life has been enriched in ways I could not have imagined through setting up my own business.

So, it is with total sincerity that I look back on my personal Tesco experience with gratitude. If I had not experienced what I did, I may never have realised the powerful drive to get away—the compulsion that propelled me into the world of a self-employed business owner.

Tesco—I say with all sincerity—thank you! I was not a good fit for you, and you were not a good fit for me. And I am perfectly okay with that.

At the same time it also saddens me to remember all those people who felt the way I did; their lives were affected detrimentally through the actions of specific leaders.

Leaders should never have an unnecessary, adverse impact on others. There will be times when people let the team or organisation down, and there will be times when we will have to tackle those who are either under-performing or sabotaging the team. As principled leaders we should strive to treat these people fairly and with the dignity that every human being deserves.

When you are really clear on your values as a leader and embed them as a foundation to your daily activities, you achieve something that is so important. You access your full potential and become the best, most authentic leader you can. As a result people follow you more readily. But it is not just your work-life that becomes better as you focus on being true to your values. Every aspect of life becomes richer.

You must be aware of your values and should review them on an annual basis as they will and do change over time. Whenever we set about identifying our values, most of us find that we very quickly identify a list of five or six that stand out above all others. But beyond this primary list there will be others that are also important to us; in my experience it is the relative importance of these primary and secondary values that changes with the passage of time.

The relative importance of my values has changed throughout my life and has driven some of my significant life choices. They changed during the period of my engagement and marriage. They changed again when my daughter was born.

The key to being true to one's values, for me, starts with my Personal Leadership Success System. This strategic method checks me in and enables me to ensure the direction I am heading in is the one aligned with who I am.

Part of this system is an annual process of reviewing and reconnecting with my values. As I review my personal values, I write them down at the front of my journal, including a few sentences below each value to reinforce and get clear about what they mean to me. Having them written in my journal means that I review them regularly and record any significant thoughts that come to mind—perhaps not every day, but a least a few days a week.

In the last few years I have realised that when I look at my values holistically they act as a compass for my life; keeping me on course and aligned to my true north. Usually, when I am not feeling good—when I can sense something in my life is not quite as it needs to be—it is because I am not being true to my values. Those occasions when I do not seem to be in the zone, when I am not in flow nor at my sharpest—it can often be because my behaviour is out of line with one or more of my values.

This level of awareness only comes from being absolutely clear on your values. It is derived from regularly reading them, seeing them or being conscious of them. When you are living in harmony with your values, you get more out of life and achieve more.

Immediately after leaving Tesco, I started work as a consultant and needed to do a lot of networking. When I started to engage with others and build a larger network of associates and contacts, I began to achieve so much more.

I was doing exactly what I had resisted at Tesco, but now I was in an environment that matched my values. I discovered that I deeply enjoyed networking, mainly due to being in an arena of my choice and living my own values.

I found myself perceiving networking in a different way to what I had been accustomed to. Now, I was having conversations with people—often very purposefully and sometimes, not so much.

I treated networking as conversation and relationship building; where I may be able to help somebody else or they may be able to help me, or neither! However a conversation unfolded, there was always the possibility that we may be able to help each other in the future.

As a leader, business owner or entrepreneur, you can deliver more through others. And it is a much more enjoyable way to do business and to live your life. Nice guys most certainly do not come last!

Our values are and should always be just that—our values. We can never live someone else's values in an honest, authentic and congruent way. Similarly, we must never seek to impose our values on others. It is beneficial, however, when we seek to share our values with those that we lead, that we take time to understand their values and identify where we have shared values.

Conversations around values and understanding what they really mean to people is an essential part of our leadership role. When individuals have clarity about their personal values, in addition to clarity around their organisation's values we achieve the highest levels of engagement.

For example, honesty can mean different things to different people. One person may have honesty as a value, one may have integrity and one may have fairness. Those three values could potentially all mean the same thing to different people or there may be close crossovers.

One's personal values really do create the foundations of how we lead. Whilst we all have different values, there are a number of values that are commonly shared, regardless of gender, nationality, race or religion.

I frequently hear people talking about honesty, fairness, trust, respect and family as personal values, these are the top five shared values in my experience.

In my book, *Don't Just Manage—Coach!,* I describe how eagerly I embraced the GROW Model when I first started to apply it in coaching sessions. Using the GROW model in a formulaic approach, I momentarily lost sight of one of my guiding principles of leadership.

Leadership is not about what you do, it is about who you are and the values that define you. I had slipped into the trap of doing leadership—applying a model in a really rigid way that was not working for me or my team.

The irony of this particular moment in my career was to become apparent several years later, when I was on the receiving end of just such behaviour. A manager in Tesco applied the latest model he had learned to me, it felt inauthentic and jarred heavily with me.

The difference between this and my rather awkward first attempts at developing others with the GROW model was the underlying intention. Despite my ineptitude at using the GROW model back then, my intention was good—I was using the model to help my team, to develop them and remain in service of them.

Contrast this to the Tesco manager; he applied the *Taking People With You* model upon me, and this was exactly how it felt—as if I was having some form of agonising surgery inflicted upon me.

Was his approach to our meeting guided by his principles and the values that defined him, or was it guided by the application of somebody else's model?

Were his questions about my daughter genuine and authentic, or was he merely connecting with me so that he could then make his request; in order to get his project done and secure his promotion?

He believed in the project and thought that it would add value to the business, yet by applying that leadership model in the way that he did, he failed to take me with him. He was pushing me—nay—dragging me behind him!

This illustrates one of my core beliefs around leadership—a belief that I want to share with as many people as possible.

There are a great many leadership tools, guides and models in the world—these provide value and a way of learning a methodology.

I am not against tools or models at all, quite the contrary in fact—I like them, I understand them and there will be many out there like me who can better understand ideas and concepts through models.

However, our leadership has to be built on a foundation of understanding our values. If the basis for our leadership ethos and style is built around models we will fail.

It is akin to trying to build a model aeroplane without understanding gravity. We can keep launching it into the air, but unless we understand the forces acting upon it, the plane will keep crashing down. We can throw it harder and harder and yes, it will keep coming down.

Each of us must understand the principles of leadership, in addition to our own values if we are to fly as leaders, if we are to enable our teams to fly.

Models help us when we are clear on the values that enable us to choose what fits with our ethos. There will be some tools and models that we come across that will jar with us and this is fine—this clarity around our values helps us make that choice. We may use the tool or model, we may discard it or we may adapt it.

The pace of technological and social change in the world will propel coaching into the echelons of key leadership skills. Soon, we shall be leading teams of far greater diversity, with wildly different aspirations for their career. Our team may include a sixteen-year-old school leaver and a seventy-year-old, because most of us will be working much longer.

Technological and social changes will increasingly bring about challenges that we have never experienced before. There was a time when our route to management or leadership was based purely on our technical expertise. We would have encountered most of the challenges that our people asked us about. The future is very different, so if we are going to help our teams solve challenges that neither we, nor they, have experienced before, we will have to rely on our coaching skills.

These beliefs have led me to work with hundreds of managers and leaders over the last few years; helping them incorporate the skills of a coach into their leadership style. As part of these programmes, I will often include some sessions around managing performance and providing great feedback.

I will often reference Ken Blanchard's *One Minute Manager* book and model in these sessions, as it is one of the seminal works in this area—a valuable model due to its simplicity and that it is centred around genuinely wanting to help people be the best that they can be.

Mission: Leadership

There is often one element that jars for some people—this could be that it is not British! The process for giving quick praise and developmental feedback involves some form of physical contact—a shaking of hands, a tap on the back or an arm on the shoulder.

This sits well with me if I do it in my own way. However, if physical contact does not work for you, simply skip that part.

It is important to know our people and understand how we can best communicate with them. In this particular context there will be individuals who respond well to physical connection and others who do not. As a leader wanting to praise and encourage it is vital that we present the praise and encouragement in ways that suit them best and which are also congruent for ourselves. Applying a model blindly without regard for the people in front of us is not the act of a leader.

Identifying a great leader from history or business is also rarely a great starting point when developing ourselves as leaders. Particularly if we are not yet clear on our own values.

In leadership courses across the UK you will hear names such as Winston Churchill, Mother Teresa and Richard Branson shouted out. Unless your values are identical to theirs, their behaviour and actions may not be suitable for you. You are almost certainly operating in a different environment to them, which influences how successful you will be in replicating what they did.

Start with a deep understanding of what is important to you, then choose the models that fit with who you are and what you believe. Then, and only then, apply them with what I describe as the *Butterfly Principle*.

Imagine that you are holding a very rare butterfly in your hand. You are trying to protect it by moving it to a safe place where it can continue to live and thrive.

If you were to hold that precious butterfly too tightly in your hand then you would crush it and kill it. You would destroy the very thing you were seeking to

nurture and hold dear. If you were to hold that butterfly too loosely in your hand, it would fly away. You would lose that most precious of things that you were seeking to help and protect.

The same is true of any leadership model that you experience and decide to use. Hold onto the model too tightly, apply it too rigidly and you will undermine your credibility as a leader—you will appear inauthentic and deceptive. Your people will feel manipulated by having leadership done to them.

When you hold onto a leadership tool or model too loosely, some of your activities or conversations will lack the structure and purpose needed for them to succeed.

This was my personal experience with the GROW model. Now, I use it as a loose framework—one that enables me be more intentional as a coach. It lets me be the best, most authentic version of me when I am coaching others.

Chapter Summary

1. As leaders we must be clear on our personal values.

2. Clarity around our personal values allows us to be the leader that we truly want to be.

3. We must review our values annually as they change over time.

4. When we are clear on our values they become our life compass—a warning system when we need to make a change.

5. When we work in an environment where we can be true to our own values we tend to perceive events and life much more positively.

6. When teams discuss and identify shared values they perform at a much higher level.

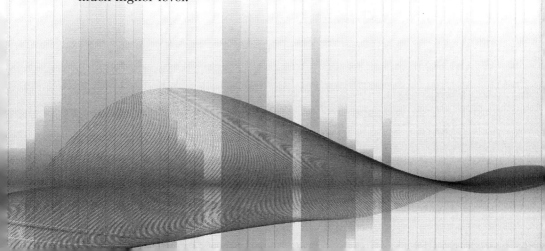

Principle Four—
Honesty and integrity are
at the core of great leadership

- Leaders must be clear on their own values but all must act with honesty and integrity.
- Honesty and integrity build trust—the band that holds teams together and allows greatness.

As a long-time advocate of *The Leadership Challenge*, Jim Kouzes and Barry Posner's book, I find it to be an absolutely essential guide for those who lead others. As one of the best leadership books ever written, the revolutionary advice presented in its pages is a valuable addition to every leader's expertise.

The authors invested over thirty years conducting surveys. These asked followers or constituents, in their own terms, what characteristics they most admired in, and wanted from their leaders.

Kouzes and Posner uncovered the top four factors that followers have consistently expressed as essential from their leaders.

Whilst working for Tesco, I was invited on a train the trainer course; an event focused on influence skills for senior managers. The external trainer was none other than my now good friend and business partner, Richard Nugent.

When I first heard the top four characteristics they did not sit well with me— actually this is an understatement, because my inner monologue was screaming that the list was wrong.

The number one thing was certainly wrong! Yes, honesty (being congruent), is really important, but the number one thing is integrity. From all my leadership training in the army this was the absolute bedrock. This was what I believed and it had served me well. Yes, I was sure that honesty was wrong!

I now realise words mean very different things to different people—one person's definition of honesty can be very close indeed to another's definition of integrity.

When working with teams and organisations on the importance of values, any discussion is moot without an exploration around what the value (and the word you associate with it) means for you. The aim of this is not to agree on shared values' words, but simply to express one's own experience of the value behind the word.

As I developed a greater understanding of my own values and beliefs, along with a finer appreciation of the research behind Kouzes and Posner's book, I found reconciling my integrity with their honesty much easier.

Honesty is not simply telling the truth or not telling a lie—honesty in this respect is about being clear on what you stand for and articulating this to those that you lead. This results in those we lead knowing what to expect of us and how we are likely to respond in a given situation.

More significantly, when people are clear on what we stand for, they will gain an insight into the resulting actions we take as leaders. This is particularly important when we have to make tough decisions; decisions that possibly make their lives uncomfortable in the short term.

Honesty is about helping others understand why we have made the tough, necessary decisions rather than easy, but wrong decisions. In my own world view, this is what I call integrity.

Throughout my seven-year journey towards becoming an officer in the army I had a lot of time to think about what I would do when I finally made it as a commissioned officer. At every step, I was hungry for information and sought out wise counsel from serving officers, senior NCOs and academics.

Sage advice that I heard over and over again was...

"Respect is hard earned but easily lost"

And...

"It takes a long time to earn the respect of those that you lead, but it can be lost in an instant."

There is a lot of wisdom in these statements, however, they do paint a bleaker picture than I believe to be true. As leaders we must strive to be respected by those that we lead, rather than simply being liked.

As leaders, to be respected by all and liked by some is much better than to be liked by all and respected by some. The former may be a lonely position at times, but that is the mantle that we carry as leaders.

Think back to Louise, from the chapter *The Answers are Not Enough,* and the challenges she faced taking over from a leader who had very much been the mother hen figure of the team. He had taken over most of the roles in the team, doing everything. On the surface it seemed as though he had been loved and respected, he was actually part of the problem.

Part of Louise's challenge, based upon her perceptions of her predecessor, was that deep down she wanted to be liked by everyone in her team. The desire to be liked is a fundamental human response that we all have—leaders have it too.

Great leaders are not narcissistic and emotionally cold; quite the opposite. Acting with integrity and being respected is far more important to great leaders—this approach has superior long-term results in every aspect of work.

The irony of Louise's situation was that her previous manager's style involved doing everything for his team and focusing on being liked—this led to him exclusively retaining most of the key knowledge about delivering essential tasks. Yet, he never tackled poor performance or challenged incongruous behaviour because he wanted to be liked.

After he left, the team began to unravel at lightning speed and Louise was left to pick up the pieces; she bore the brunt of what he had sown.

Can respect be lost in an instant? Maybe, maybe not. As leaders we are still human, we still have the same range of human emotions, desires and needs as everyone else. We can still be found wanting at times and we make mistakes.

The job of a leader is to strive to do the right thing, always in the knowledge that we do not operate in a black and white environment. Sometimes, the right thing to do is a shade of grey and the answer is not clear cut.

A single mistake in judgement can undermine you as a leader but it may not necessarily destroy you. Therefore, this scenario is not as dire as these statements suggest.

If we invest our time striving to be the best we can be—if we seek to protect and serve those we lead—they will forgive us the odd slip-up! As long as we strive to rectify the situation, affording them the same courtesy and leeway, you can heal the relationship.

It is not the making of a mistake that is the crime. The crime is failing to admit our mistakes, not putting things right and then not seeking to learn from them. Without this, we are modelling a set of behaviours where mistakes are hidden. This creates a culture of fear that is inherently risk averse, and that never leads to optimal performance.

I am testament to the ethos that respect is not always totally lost in one error of judgement. There is one personal failing from my leadership career that I still frequently reflect upon, over a decade later.

As a young officer in the army I made an insignificant and almost inconsequential mistake in front of my soldiers. I asked them not mention this to anybody—as loyal and trusted members of my troop, they did indeed maintain their silence. Nevertheless, I should not have asked that of them.

This harmless, personal mistake may have caused my credibility to take a little knock but it certainly did not destroy it. It may even have shown me in a more human light to my soldiers.

They knew that I cared about them and that I put their needs ahead of my own at all times, except for the rarest of occasions.

I was not the epitome of perfection as an army officer. I did not win the Sword of Honour at Sandhurst nor did I graduate at the top of my class. However, I strived to lead my soldiers; to be of service to them—when it came to the real test, this was what mattered most to them.

My best friend and I often joke that we have consistently been in the bottom of the top third in all that we do—be that at Sandhurst or in any sporting events that we have entered. I share this with you intentionally and humbly, for to inspire people towards achieving amazing results, you do not need to be an incredible member of the leadership elite.

I graduated Sandhurst, positioned in that aforementioned bottom of the top third, yet I was a good army officer. When I asked my soldiers to lift their masks for me, they did so without hesitation. You too can get people to lift their masks for you by being intentional about your leadership.

Many believe leadership to be a lonely and tough job at times, which can be true in certain circumstances, but that is the exception rather than the rule. In twenty years of leadership positions, I have had the profound privilege to lead great teams and help them achieve more than we ever thought possible. That has been great fun, has built lasting friendships and I have loved it.

There are times we need to make tough calls and this can give the impression of a lonely path, although we rarely make these decisions by ourselves. Building a great team around us with an open, trusting set of relationships enables leaders to meet those decisions as a team.

We leaders do not need to have all of the answers... The toughest decisions in my career have involved circumstances as far removed as defending a port in southern Iraq and how to communicate another set of redundancies. These, and other difficult choices, have been made with my team.

Whilst the final decisions rested on my shoulders, I was never lonely, because I included my team of trusted advisors. Even when they disagreed with my final decision, they felt valued and understood why I arrived at that decision—because they were included in the process.

People often say that anyone can sail a boat in calm seas, but it is a true skipper who can sail a boat in stormy waters. The same is true of leadership.

Leading a team when all is well—when you have a high-performing team and market conditions in your favour—is not that challenging. The real test of our abilities as leaders comes when conditions are tough, the competition is fierce and the environmental factors appear to be conspiring against your every move.

These are the times when we really step up to the plate and lead—when our personal values and our commitment to act with honesty and integrity must be relied upon. For it is in these moments when we are forced to choose between the hard, right decisions and the easy, wrong decisions.

Some of these decisions will be difficult for people to accept, as they are not the outcome they wanted. However, they will accept them if they know why we have made them, what we stand for and that we always act consistently.

Chapter Summary

1. As leaders we must identify our own leadership philosophy, based upon our own values and beliefs.

2. Seeking to mimic the actions of other leaders can be a risky strategy.

3. Honesty is about being clear on what we stand for and articulating this to those that we lead.

4. Trust and respect must be built over time. We cannot *expect* others to trust and respect us.

5. Trust and respect are not always totally lost in one single instance or error of judgement.

6. As leaders we are human and will make mistakes, but it is our duty to admit them, put them right and learn from them.

7. If we concentrate on building a great team, leadership is rarely a lonely job.

8. Acting with honesty and integrity helps others to understand our actions when we have to make tough, unpopular decisions.

Principle Five—
Protect and care for
those you lead

- Leadership is about relationships; which must be built and nurtured with intentionality.

- People will do incredible things when they know that their leaders know and care about them. When they feel safe.

- Everybody that we lead is the most important person in the world to somebody and our actions as leaders impact people's whole life—not just their work life.

For a number of years, I have trained and mentored various groups of businesspeople on leadership and coaching programmes. With such a wealth of skill and business expertise in these groups, I have taken the opportunity to ask about the best leaders people have worked with or encountered.

This question has elicited many responses, with a few predominant themes becoming apparent. There was one particular answer that was given without fail and it is this quality which differentiates good leaders and great leaders.

One of the most powerful factors that causes leaders to stand out as the best, is time. In every occasion and in each group, at least two or three people have offered, completely unprompted, that what made these leaders more striking than any other was their generosity in the amount of time they gave.

This is usually articulated in a number of different ways from those who simply say, "They made time for me," to those who say that their best ever leader never cancelled a one-to-one.

At the very moment of this comment, somebody usually replies very despondently that they have never had a one-to-one with their manager. As they utter those words, their body language visibly closes and sinks–the sadness can be heard in their voice at the realisation that their leader does not care. And this makes me sad.

Leaders who demonstrate this giving of time for their team members, are extraordinary examples of those who protect and care for those who they lead.

I would always make time for the soldiers whom I had the privilege to lead in the army. Be that crawling into the shell scrape with them on a cold rainy night in Wales or, as a young platoon commander, talking to them about their families. I invested a great deal of my time in developing their careers and helping them to grow. I believe that my soldiers followed me on operations because they knew I cared about them.

When I left the military and entered into the corporate world, I was determined to replicate this behaviour with my new team, ensuring that I keep time with them sacrosanct. I would ensure that we always had one-to-one time and I would offer them time to talk about their agenda first.

Different people in my team needed different amounts of my time, at different stages. The same will be true with those that you lead–you will have some that need and want very little time, whilst others need more.

This will usually depend on the situation and circumstances; a team member may not require much time on one occasion, yet six months down the line, when they take on a new role or more responsibility, they want and need more.

Be intentional about investing time in your team–employ that time to appreciate their needs and also use it to grow as a leader yourself. If you have led your team for a considerable length of time you can still do this. Set up sessions with your team members with a view to exploring aspects of what you do and ask yourself some probing questions.

- If we were coming at this fresh what would we do?
- If we were consultants looking at this, what would we suggest?
- If we were rebuilding this team from scratch, what would we do?
- If we knew nothing about the history of this team, what would we ask?

And if you are concerned about what you team might think—be honest. For instance, your team would respect you for saying, "I'd like to understand more about your challenges so that I can better support you. Can I come to that meeting with you?"

This will not be viewed as lack of trust or micromanagement; it will demonstrate that you care. The best leaders I have ever worked with, worked for, coached or trained, understand on a deeper level than most that real leaders care.

Leadership is not about the application of tools or models (although they can help when built upon the foundation of genuinely caring about those that you lead). Leadership is about being of service to the team—this is achieved only by caring about them.

When people have a sense that their leaders really know them, they feel safe at work and they feel safe around their leaders. Think about the people that you trust the most or feel the safest around. I am certain you will be thinking of your closest friends and family members.

The reason you feel so safe around friends and family is because they truly know who you are and accept you for it. They are the people who know who you are when the work-mask drops away.

Why is this so important for leaders? When people feel safe they will work for you with blood, sweat and tears—they will go the extra mile and they will do what you ask of them because they want to, not just because you tell them to.

As leaders we have a huge duty of care to those in our charge. People have feelings and emotions; they are the most important people in somebody else's life, be that their spouse, partner, son, daughter or any other relation or friend.

What we do as leaders has a huge impact on the lives of those that we lead and those closest to them. Regardless of our seniority, when leading people, our impact reaches beyond the confines of the organisation and those who work for us.

Most people can relate to the aspiration of treating others how you would like to be treated. However, our responsibilities as leaders go a little deeper, because our actions touch the lives of many people. The adage for leaders is really...

Treat others how we would like to be treated and how we would like our loved ones to be treated.

Most have encountered leaders who bark instructions at their teams without courtesy, politeness or gratitude. We all have experience of leaders who just want the work done, regardless of what the team member has on their plate. You may also have heard the phrase *JFDI* being used once or twice!

If we are being completely honest, we have all said and done some of these things ourselves on occasion, whilst coming close on that continuum of attitudes and behaviours at other times.

We spend as much time (and in some instances, more), with our work colleagues as we do with our friends and family. This means how we are as leaders has an enormous influence on the lives of other people.

We do not need to be the best friend of everyone that we lead—in fact, a degree of healthy separation is often important. Yet, there is no need to bark orders like the stereotypical sergeant major.

I certainly avoided this during my army career. There were times when we were under pressure and I needed people to respond quickly to a very real threat. In these instances there may have been some distinctly canine sounds being made, but this was not my instinctual methodology.

The corporate world generally does not face the same ultimate threat or outcomes when things go wrong. Rarely are we in a situation where people's lives are on the line. Nevertheless, I have seen and experienced leaders in the civilian world who bark orders as if they are under fire.

There is always scope to request, rather than demand, just as there is always time to express gratitude. The need for manners and civility is paramount, regardless of how busy we are.

These behaviours go a very long way to creating profound levels of motivation within those we lead. They also have a huge impact on the families of those we lead.

An illustration of the value this principle offers us comes from an instant when I did not remain true to my own values and principles. This came about during a coaching session in the early part of my career—it was a session that I still regret.

As the session progressed, I failed to challenge my client enough; ultimately the impact was that I did not add much value to my client or his business. However, it was a powerful lesson for me; one that made me even clearer about my personal coaching style and the strength of my core beliefs surrounding leadership.

My client was the MD and part owner of a small, yet profitable business. He was incredibly driven and highly capable as an entrepreneur and salesman. I was in awe of his tenacity and the anecdotes of how he got his products listed in some of the UK's largest supermarkets.

I was coaching him in the development of his leadership capability. He felt that his small team were not as committed as he was, that they did not demonstrate the same drive and that they failed to grasp the impact their actions were having on the business' success.

At one point in our conversation we were talking about the team, how well he knew them and how well they knew him. During this conversation he said something that shocked me—I knew it was a major limiting belief, yet I chose not to explore it with him.

It was a comment that struck at the heart of all I knew to be true about leadership. Perhaps back then I had not analysed my own career in as much depth as I have now, so I may not have consciously known quite how significant it was. Yet, I knew it was significant and I chose not to act.

He said to me, "Ben, I don't care about their lives outside of work so long as they come here and work hard for me."

Embedded deep within that statement is the very thing that enables some leaders to galvanise a team to walk through walls for them, whilst others instil a desperate need to visit a pub!

When those we lead know that we care about them they will do incredible things for us—as those two soldiers did when I asked them to lift their masks.

Those two men lifted their masks for their fellow soldiers, not just for me. However, strong leadership from me and my fellow officers created a culture, an environment and a team whereby people would feel able to do that for each other. A culture where people will work with all they have to give, including their lives, for each other as well as for their leaders.

Culture is a function of leadership—the culture of any team, department, division or company is always a function of leadership. It is a direct result of how its leaders behave, and their behaviour needs to be congruent with their word.

When people get a sense that we know and value them then they feel safe and they trust us. This is key—when people feel safe and trusted they will follow their leaders and do incredible things for them.

The opposite is also true. If those that we lead believe that we are failing to care about them or that we are only showing care because we were told to do so on a leadership course, they will see us as dishonest. They will question our morals, values and integrity, a mindset that is hard to reverse or change.

When people operate in this environment or have these perceptions of us as leaders, they will do what we ask, but never anything beyond that. They are likely to do the absolute minimum in order to keep their jobs, but they certainly would not lift their masks for each other or for us as leaders.

Chapter Summary

1. Great leaders give their time generously to those they lead.

2. Giving your time as a leader shows that you truly care.

3. People feel safe at work when they know their leaders care.

4. When people feel safe they will work for us with blood, sweat and tears—willingly going the extra mile.

5. How we act as leaders has an impact on those we lead and their close friends and family.

6. There is always scope to request as opposed to demand.

7. Manners and civility are paramount; regardless of how busy we are.

8. Culture is a function of leadership; the result of how the leaders in an organisation behave.

Principle Six—
Leadership is about others, but it starts with us

- In order to serve to lead, we must look after ourselves.
- Our own physical, mental, emotional and spiritual health is critically important to our success as leaders.
- Those that we lead will follow our example; good or bad.

Caring for our own health is an aspect of leadership that many people find challenging. I found looking after myself a real struggle at various points in my career; from getting hypothermia during army training, to the significant stresses during my time at Tesco. These experiences have given me a great deal of empathy for leaders who seek out coaching for support with work-life balance.

In some respects, the difficulties in taking care of oneself as a corporate employee seem obvious—between deadline-driven time constraints, workload and managerial pressure, it is easy to see why people can be stressed or suffer ill health in that environment.

When it comes to being self-employed, it seems paradoxical that I would have such difficulty looking after my health, when I was my own boss. I could take time to exercise, prepare healthy food and decide when, where and how I worked. Nevertheless, it took me a good eighteen months to strike a balance with a maintainable, weekly regime.

I felt that it should be much easier than Tesco or even the army, because I had a choice—carte blanche in every aspect of my life, both personally and professionally. What I failed to realise in the early days of running a business is that we all wrestle with similar demons.

We try to rationalise how taking care of ourselves will damage us in other areas, such as...

If I go to the gym at lunchtime my boss will think I'm not committed!

What will my boss do if I don't respond to his 7am email, because I'm out jogging?

Will it damage my career if I... Yes! I think it will.

...translate into...

If I go for a bike ride now and can't get to my phone in time, I might miss out on new clients!

What will happen to my reputation if clients leave bad reviews, because I didn't get back to them at the weekend?

Will my business fail if I... Yes! I think it will.

Every single one of these is a lie; actually they are all the same lie!

We are bombarded with information about job security, redundancy, recession, technology negating human jobs, competition from overseas' freelancers, and various other aspects of the current business climate that cause people to fear for their jobs.

It is a similar experience for those who are running their own company. There is a consistent message that to be successfully self-employed you must work eighteen-hour days for five years, sacrificing your friends, family, health, hobbies, and only then you can enjoy the rewards.

It is all rubbish, but for me it seemed so real—my reality was filled with the same fears, worries, and assumptions as many of those in a corporate environment. I immediately checked my emails on waking, then sat at the kitchen table from 8am prompt. I would hardly move from that position until after 5pm, when I collected my daughter from nursery.

My back would be sore, I was always tired and brain-fried; without meetings or conversation with colleagues to distract me, I had plenty of focused, productive time... except I was not productive. The same fears that kept me constantly doing work, were stopping me from being a successful businessperson.

If you are unable to care for yourself, you cannot look after those you are leading—even if this is just yourself! You do not need to be a triathlete or marathon runner; there is no need to go to the gym five days a week, but physical fitness is important.

Having a balanced degree of physical fitness will facilitate better leadership, as it allows us to be more resilient and cope with periods of intense pressure. Leaders who pay attention to their own health and well-being tend to be the ones who can remain calm in a crisis, continue to make sound decisions supporting their teams, whilst those around them are losing their heads.

Sleep is another vital requirement of good health and excellence in leadership. According to the neuroscientist, Dr Tara Swart, just four hours of sleep loss can have the same impairment on cognitive brain function as coming into work having just drunk a six-pack of beer!

A disturbed night's sleep can reduce a person's IQ by five to eight points. Knowing this has led me to view those who brag about sleep deprivation as a sign of their toughness as rather misguided. Leaders who wear lack of sleep as a badge of honour, put their organisation at risk and are failing to demonstrate the necessary duty of care they have for their teams.

And it is not just sleep that is important to us—when we are dehydrated we decrease our cerebral function. This means a mere 1% loss of hydration, can significantly affect decision-making abilities and mental capacity.

Yet most of us do not drink enough water to stay fully hydrated throughout the day, especially in the drying atmosphere of an air-conditioned office. If you consider that thirst is an indicator of poor hydration—by the time you feel thirsty you are probably already 1-3% dehydrated.

Hunger can also be a sign of dehydration, with many people misinterpreting their body's need for more fluids as an indicator to eat, rather than drink. A glass of water at the first sign of hunger will help differentiate between thirst and genuine need for food. As a very rough guide, you should be drinking around half a litre of water for every fifteen kilogrammes of body weight per day, more if you exercise regularly.

If we are going to lead others to the best of our ability, and truly serve to lead, then we must look after ourselves. In this respect, taking care of our own health and well-being becomes a critically important leadership skill. My colleague, Richard Nugent, believes it is a strategic imperative that you (and if you are senior enough, the rest of your management team) are in reasonable physical condition.

The words *strategic imperative* may seem extreme to some, but they are true. Even the most amazing business leaders are useless when they are ill or dead. Whether you choose to use these words or not, the key thing is a plan and dedicated focus. It is all too easy for us to neglect exercise, in whatever form works for us, when we are really busy and under pressure.

The paradox comes in times when we really believe we do not have time to exercise—these are the occasions we really need to make time to exercise. Robin Sharma once said that he who fails to make time for exercise will eventually have to make time for sickness.

A leader's job is to lead by example and set the standards of behaviour for others to follow. We must therefore make a conscious effort to be an inspiring role model for those we lead; embodying the behaviours we know will deliver results—the results our business or department is responsible for. At the same time we must show we care about our team—that we are not willing to sacrifice their well-being for the task.

The ten principles of leadership within this book will help you act from a perspective of leadership, rather than simply doing leadership models. What are harder to identify and accept, are the behaviours we display as leaders that demonstrate the wrong example. Like it or not, we all have them. These are the shadow that we cast as opposed to the light that we shine.

For instance, if we go on holiday for two weeks and regularly send or respond to emails, our people will assume we expect this of them—whether that is our true intention or not. If we send emails at 6am and 9pm each day, our people will believe this is required to be successful in the company. So, this will become the culture that exists across the organisation.

The behaviour sends the message that switching off and recharging is not really important. Worse still, if we are telling our people they should switch off, yet refuse to do so ourselves, we are not being honest and we are not being congruent.

Due to my naivety and desire for success, there were occasions at World Challenge when I stayed late in the office because Nigel, the managing director, was still there. On occasions there was a genuine reason; I needed to discuss a matter with him and when most people had gone home was a good time to catch him.

At other times I waited around deliberately because I could discuss non-work-related topics and strengthen our relationship. Yet there were times I would hang around, just because he was in the office and I thought that was what I should be doing also.

The reality was, at points I was not very productive because I was tired. Then, on the next day I would be unfocused because I had stayed until late—I was following the example that I was set.

As leaders, our role is to inspire and uplift those around us. We must leave those we encounter with a greater sense of energy than when we met. In this respect we seek to inspire, motivate and encourage.

The majority of people can think of at least one mood-hoover they have encountered in their career— the person with the ability to suck the life out of the room as soon as they enter. That is not leadership. We need to intentionally radiate an attitude that lifts people up and impacts their lives in beneficial ways.

However, as leaders we do not need to be superhuman or never have a bad day. We simply need to manage our energy levels, mood and state; understanding the impact they have on our team.

Looking after our physical, mental and emotional health means we come to work as the best version of ourselves, ready to inspire others.

When training to become an army officer, I overheard a colleague say that complaints always go up the chain of command and never down. It made me smile when a few years later I heard the same phrase used in the film *Saving Private Ryan*.

If we are having a tough day, then it is important for us to have a safe outlet for our frustrations. That may be a close colleague or peer, perhaps even our boss. And if we are frustrated with another individual (or one of our colleagues), we absolutely must ensure that these gripes never go down the organisational structure.

Gripes always go up the command chain, never down.

Chapter Summary

1. Do not believe the myths. You do not need to sacrifice your health, friends, family and social life to be successful in work or in business.

2. If you do not look after yourself, you cannot look after those you lead.

3. Getting enough quality sleep is critically important in order for us to be effective leaders.

4. Being in reasonable physical condition is a strategic imperative.

5. The times when we think we do not have time to exercise are the times when we most need to make time to exercise.

6. People will follow the example we set as leaders; good or bad.

7. Our state influences the state of our team. Our mood becomes the mood of our team.

Principle Seven—
Leaders do not need to
have all of the answers

- Our job as a leader is not to be the smartest person in the room with all of the answers.
- Our job as a leader is to enable others to deliver.
- Our job is to deliver through others.

Of all the principles that have served me well over the years, this was the very first I discovered. Sitting opposite a major from the British Army, listening intently to every word he said, even at fourteen years old I was captivated.

It can be very challenging at that young age for many children to visit their school's careers office and make choices that will affect the rest of their lives—for me, it was easy, because of how inspired I was at that moment.

"Ben," the major looked me directly in the eyes and said, "you do not need to have all the answers!"

Those words he spoke that day are forever etched into my mind—they have also sat at the heart of my leadership ethos ever since. It is a universally powerful lesson, yet one that so many leaders fail to grasp early enough in their careers. I consider myself fortunate to have encountered it so early on.

It truly is a game changer of epic proportions.

By appreciating, accepting and believing that you do not need to know all the answers, you give yourself permission just to lead and your team members to come into their own, using their skills and unique knowledge set.

If the thought of not having all of the answers and being involved in the details of your team's activities makes you more than a little uncomfortable, chances are that you have not fully made the transition from doer/manager to leader.

Despite your very best intentions, if you are micromanaging or have become a super-manager, some of your team members are very likely to feel stifled, because they have little autonomy at work.

When we hold onto the false belief that we must have all of the answers and make all of the decisions, we send a very clear message to our team. That message is very different to the one we intend. In this respect we can often cast a long, dark shadow over the times spent leading a team in this way.

Our misplaced desire or need to make all of the decisions can be perceived in myriad ways. These are often described as a lack of freedom, a lack of trust or having no autonomy to act.

None of these feelings are how we would want those in our charge to feel at work, however, these are the consequences when we fail to both grasp and act on this fundamental truth about leadership.

If this concept fills you with unease, you will need to get comfortable with it extremely quickly. The rate of social and technological change has accelerated hugely in the last ten years and is set to continue accelerating.

Soon we will have five generations working side by side in the workplace—all will have differing needs and aspirations. These changes in society bring fresh challenges around how we support and develop our people, challenges that we have never faced before.

The rate of technological change will force you to adapt to new technology, new channels of communication and different ways of working, that neither you nor those in your teams and organisations will have faced before.

Being able to rely on your own specific experience to answer questions your teams raise, or challenges that you collectively face, will become a rarity. In the future there will be an increased number of situations where we genuinely do not know the answer.

When this happens, we have four choices:

1. Be driven by ego and make a scientific guess (also known as a punt) and hope it works out.

2. Do nothing, wait and see what the market does, whilst hoping for the best.

3. Work out a solution with the team.

4. Delegate the decision making (with full support) to the most qualified person in the team or network.

Clearly two of these decisions create a competitive disadvantage at best and at worst consign your organisation to failure—the way so many great high street brands have gone in the last decade.

The term *VUCA* (Volatile, Uncertain, Complex and Ambiguous) has been increasingly used over the last few years; describing the world in which we now operate. At the same time, the cry goes up that we need a whole new set of leadership skills and competencies to cope in this new world.

This brings a wry smile to my face along with a degree of frustration—it is not a new concept and it does not need a whole new set of competencies!

The military have been operating in this type of environment ever since men took up arms against each other. In war, leaders at all levels of the command chain operate in this type of world.

Quite the contrary to needing a whole new set of leadership behaviours, we simply return to the fundamental principles of leadership.

We need to clearly articulate a vision of the future so that everyone knows, with total clarity, what we are working towards and where the assigned tasks fit into a broader picture.

By focusing on the building of great relationships with our teams, we achieve two things...

Firstly, it demonstrates to them, we care. When they know that, they will be more inclined to follow us, especially when we make extreme requests of them.

Next, it builds trust—they trust us and we trust them.

By accepting that we do not need to have all of the answers and make all of the decisions, we step back and take in the whole picture. When people understand the bigger picture, combined with a high level of trust in the organisation, we feel greater comfort at the prospect of delegating decision-making responsibilities to our teams.

We can give our people the freedom and autonomy to act because we trust them to do the right thing. They will want to prove our trust is well placed, in addition to understanding what they are ultimately striving to achieve.

When these factors combine into a very agile and responsive team (or organisation), you are much more effective at confusing and outmanoeuvring your competition. Your team can adapt each time the situation changes, because they understand your overall intent and they have the freedom to act.

Compare this to a low-trust organisation where people have little freedom to act or make decisions—one where leaders want to retain all the decision making themselves. To arrive at any decision, the teams are reliant on a long and convoluted communication chain—one that often exists within congested email systems.

It may take anything from several days to many weeks for an issue to be escalated appropriately, the decision to be finalised and for this decision to be communicated back down the chain.

Meanwhile, more agile competitors will have stolen the competitive advantage. Customers will have been sitting at home, getting more and more disgruntled at the poor service and slow response times. Of course, with various social media tools at their fingertips, they will not simply sit at home thinking about it!

Whilst the slow cogs of decision making start to turn in your organisation they will have posted their rant on Facebook and Twitter or uploaded their thoughts on Trip Advisor. Can you really afford to let your ego or misplaced belief—that leaders need to have all of the answers—affect your team or organisation in this way?

The leadership capability of any organisation is one of the last remaining, and sustainable, competitive advantages in business today.

When developing and mentoring leaders, I hear many people explain that they wish they had more time—this is often accompanied with the hope that their team would come to them with solutions rather than questions and problems.

"Why can't they just think for themselves?"

In so many instances, we are the problem, not them. In these scenarios we have trained them to continually come to us for the answers. As busy professionals, our focus often goes to doing things and managing things—we are deceived by the illusion that it is quicker to just tell them what to do than nurture autonomy.

We are actually training them with an expectation—we will feed them the answers, rather than enabling them to think for themselves. Although, we continue to ask why they are so reliant on us.

This methodology is akin to Pavlov training his dogs to come to the bowl when he rang the bell and then, a few weeks later asking...

"Why do the dogs come to the bowl every time I ring the bell?"

If we believe that leaders need to have all the answers we drive the behaviour of wanting to be in all the detail. Once again, when we are in all of the detail, we create the perception that we do not trust our team members.

Furthermore, by becoming swamped in the detail, we sap the time needed to plan for the future or view the bigger picture. We will not have time to plan ahead; to anticipate and remove obstacles before they become a crisis—and this is what we are paid for as leaders.

Whilst coaching and training leaders, senior leaders and senior directors in a major international business, I uncovered a common theme. Regardless of the level at which they worked, many explained the culture of the business meant they had to be concerned about all of the detail.

It was expected of them to play a part in every meeting or decision; if they failed in this endeavour it would reflect really badly on them and potentially impact their career.

Regardless of their position, people disliked how it made them feel, however, most responded to the environment by continuing to get involved in the detail.

The culture of micromanagement that had become endemic within the organisation failed to inspire anybody—it encouraged a set of behaviours where people fabricated data when put on the spot.

In that same organisation I have met a few very brave and inspiring leaders who were determined to act with integrity and do the right thing, rather than the easy thing. These individuals were clear on their values—what they stood for—and were determined to act congruently.

One such leader attended a meeting where a colleague of his was being pressured to provide a figure to their boss in a meeting. It was evident that they did not have the real number, but the pressure of the situation led them to state a number that was not accurate.

The leader knew with certainty the figure his colleague had given was wrong, and although he did not know the number himself, he spoke up. He told his boss that he could not say what the number was, however, he knew the number given was not accurate and that he could go away and retrieve it.

There have been multiple times in my career—in the army, in the corporate world or since running my own business—that I have not had the answers. In the vast majority of those situations I have asked my team for help and we reached a far better outcome than through me bluffing the answers.

Clearly, as leaders we need to make decisions ourselves—if we made a habit of continually saying, "I don't know," we would quickly undermine our credibility as a leader.

When I took on the head of HR role at World Challenge, I knew about leading and developing people, creating teams and cultures, but I knew very little about salaries.

I remained humble by asking lots of questions of my pay and benefits expert. I also made a conscious effort to be curious about her role, asking her to explain each aspect to me and using my intellect to understand what she was saying. At any juncture, if things did not make sense I would ask. If I was not entirely sure what she explained was the best or only solution I would ask more questions.

Rather than saying I did not have a clue, I asked questions—this created trust, as well as engagement, showing them in a tangible way how much I valued them.

In the army, I would never just roll up and tell a new group of soldiers that I was the boss and I knew what was best for them. When joining a team at Tesco, I did not sit back and explain that I knew nothing about online learning.

These approaches originate in ego and can present the appearance of you not caring for the team, because it is all about you. This is arrogance, not leadership! When you let go of ego and the need to know all the answers, you develop better listening skills. Letting go of every encounter being about you, you free up headspace to truly lead your team.

You are never seeking to become the expert in each of your team member's roles—this is what they are employed to do! You are simply looking to grasp the basics; enough to ask the right questions, positively challenge and coach for success.

Remember, those that we lead want us to be competent as leaders, not necessarily the expert in every role. Our expertise is in enabling the team to make the very best decisions. This is very different from us having all the expert knowledge to have every answer.

When we include our team, listen to their ideas and demonstrate that we truly value their intellect, we build huge amounts of trust. This only comes from letting go of our ego and the idea that we need to have all of the answers.

Chapter Summary

1. Leaders do not need to have all of the answers.

2. Accepting that we do not need to have all of the answers is a leadership game changer.

3. When we hold on to all decision making, it sends the message that we do not trust our team members.

4. The ability to lead based on our technical experience and expertise, will significantly diminish in the near future.

5. A VUCA world does not require a whole new set of leadership skills; it requires a return to the fundamental principles of leadership.

6. Trust and autonomy create an agile team that can out-think and out-manoeuvre your competition.

7. A leader's job is to be an expert in leadership. It is not our job to be an expert in what our team members do.

Principle Eight—
Strive for Mastery

- The best leaders are insatiable learners.
- Leaders should continually seek to develop themselves and everyone in their team or organisation, be they leaders or functional specialists.
- The most dangerous time for any leader is the moment that they think they or their organisation has nothing left to learn. Nothing fails like success.

Competency has consistently been ranked in the top qualities that people most want from their leaders. This competence in leadership is ranked more highly, and is more important to those we lead, than being a functional expert in our specialist field prior to becoming a leader.

And here exists an intriguing paradox...

Most of us have invested deeply into developing our technical expertise, through training courses, reading, practice, feedback from our bosses or peers and so on. Contrast that with how much time we invest in developing our skills and mastery of leadership and for many there will be a striking difference!

Yet when we become leaders, when we accept the responsibility of leadership, those that we lead want our expertise in this area much more than our technical ability. In the military, officers are trained to be leaders—their investment of time learning technical expertise is almost entirely based in leadership.

The most dangerous time for any leader or organisation is that period when they feel they have nothing left to learn. We can all recall examples of once great companies; the industry leaders, once at the top of their game, who suddenly disappeared from the stock market.

This was partly due to their complacency—they assumed they had nothing left to learn. Nokia, RIM and Kodak are just a few examples of those companies whose failure to keep learning caused them to fall behind the ever-changing world.

The military operates in a very unique environment, whereby its role in peacetime is largely to train for operations. It requires the necessary investment of time and funding. The British Army is so effective when deployed on active duty is because it is always training, learning and developing.

Leaders at all levels of the command structure are constantly practising their leadership skills, refining them and learning more. This is what makes them extremely successful.

The same is true in the sporting world, where world class athletes and elite sports teams share a number of mindsets and thought processes with the military.

One of these is their approach to learning and feedback—their hunger for knowledge and learning does not diminish with time. It is quite the opposite. The better they get the hungrier they are for knowledge and further development. This is what makes them great and often sets them apart from their competitors.

England Rugby, under the leadership of Sir Clive Woodward, had a philosophy of seeking out a hundred 1% improvements that they knew would add up to World Cup victory—which it did.

These are now well known and documented, including considerations such as a clean kit at half time, working with an eye-training specialist, rubber spots on their shirts to help the ball stick, laptops for all players so that they could communicate and a strictly enforced team charter to name a few.

There are numerous examples from the world of sport and business where teams have achieved great success through concentrating on a large number of small, incremental improvements (marginal gains).

In my experience developing high-performing teams around the world and studying the greatest teams from both sport and business, there are a number of common themes that stand out.

World class teams constantly strive for mastery and have a consistent focus on teamwork, how they are working as a team.

Compare this to the average team which has meetings dominated by tasks and what needs to be done. The average team consigns team development to an annual chore, often conducted off-site, swinging from trees. This is not an effective team development strategy.

If you want your team to be one of the best teams in the world, then you need to be prepared to adopt the ethos of those teams that focus on and pay attention to team development.

At TwentyOne Leadership we have a constant agenda item, one of the first on the agenda that says *Ways of Working*. This reminds us that we need to constantly be cultivating teamwork and how we are operating.

This can be as simple as a quick discussion to remind ourselves to stay connected during particularly busy times and make a commitment to doing so. On other occasions one of us shares some new learning and we discuss the application of it for us as a team, or our clients. These discussions have led to some notable performance shifts for us.

One such shift came from discussing Patrick Lencioni's book, *The Five Dysfunctions of a Team*. We explored our own individual feelings about conflict and constructive challenge, to know more clearly how comfortable we all were.

Simply sharing our different perspectives has enabled us to have much more open and frank conversations—these, in turn, have delivered much better outcomes. Sometimes we have developed a new plan or strategy, whilst at other times it has meant one of us was able to say what we really thought (knowing the team had listened and ultimately disagreed), yet fully commit.

Investing in personal development is not merely centred on financial investment. It is also investing your time and focus in whatever way works for you. Frequently, investing the time is more significant than the money.

Investment could take the form of courses, seeking a coach or mentor, reading, networking, joining a mastermind group, using social media, attending conferences or just dedicating time to reflect on your leadership journey.

Robin Sharma often says that to treble your income, you should double your investment in learning. Whilst I cannot testify to the amounts, I absolutely commit to the sentiment. My colleagues and I at TwentyOne Leadership have pledged to invest around 10% of our profits each year back into our own development. We know it is one of the differences that make a difference.

Corporate learning is often concerned with the need and challenge of measuring the return on investment. Depending on the learning context, this is sometimes important and worthwhile; sometimes it is not.

With regards to my personal learning and drive for mastery, I long ago stopped thinking about return on investment. Not because I fail to see its importance—quite the contrary—I know that there is always a pay-off, even if this is not a direct, linear or therefore, obvious relationship.

I have discovered the return on the investment often comes from a different place to where one might expect; and often it is many years down the line.

One of the most profound aspects of my own investment in personal development (and those in my teams whose development I have supported), is the connection made with other people. The benefit of investing in development is often as much about these connections, as it is about the content.

The opportunity to learn from your peers is often hugely undervalued. As is talking with people facing similar challenges in different organisations or even hearing about the challenges they are facing. Maybe you have faced that challenge previously and can help them, or perhaps it will help you several months, or years later, when you face a related challenge.

One valuable learning that I relied upon in the army (something I forgot for a while in my corporate life), was the degree of value leaders can deliver through others. This is achieved by engaging them in our vision, connecting with them and inspiring them. If we fail to do this, we are micromanaging them or being a super-manager, which are both short-term strategies.

The connections I have formed through investing time and money in personal development have helped me throughout my career with various projects. As leaders we are often only as good as the strength of our network and relationships, within and outside of the organisation we work for.

I regularly attend a one-day leadership conference in London called *BenchMark for Business* and it would be easy to say that I cannot find the time to go, once a quarter. I have heard many speakers at the conference who have inspired me, challenged me to think differently about my business and been the catalyst to adjust my strategy.

I have been exposed to some of the greatest minds in leadership, science and psychology—this has enhanced my knowledge and allowed me to better serve my clients, which in itself is incredibly valuable.

At that conference I have made new contacts who have helped me with projects for my clients, plus I have introduced others to my contacts, leading to work for them. I have met and spoken with some amazing business leaders, some of whom have helped me with the creation of this book.

It was Jim Rohn who once said, "You are the average of the five people you spend the most time with." Based on this sentiment, I want to hang out with and learn from people who inspire me; those who are pushing the boundaries in all aspects of their life.

The other reason that I stopped worrying about the return on my personal investment in learning, is that I found the application of learning often takes a meandering path.

This is not simply an instance of going on that course, learned x and now I'm doing y. Sometimes I attended a course, learned x and a year later was facing a conundrum of sorts and remembered to do y! This is still hugely valuable to me, though perhaps more significant, is the amalgamation of learning.

I have found that by investing in personal development I have developed a huge melting pot of knowledge and ideas. Partially through a natural, unconscious process of assimilating new knowledge and creating my own application of it.

This unconscious process is aided by journaling—part of my Personal Leadership Success System—which was partly brought about through this very process and certainly came about through investing in personal development.

The final phase in the amalgamation of my Personal Leadership Success System came from hearing Phil Jones, MD of Brother UK, speak at a conference in London. His keynote was different to most of the speakers who present at that particular conference and it struck a chord with me for a number of reasons.

He regularly attends the conference himself as a delegate and understood the need to invest in his development as a leader. He presented his own, personal leadership modus operandi, which was an amalgamation of everything he has heard, read or learned over the years.

The most transformative aspect of this for me was that he had moulded them into his own system. He found a way to take what he had learned, what fitted with his values, and use it in a way that was authentically him. Making him the best version of himself as a leader.

The wisdom I experienced at that conference inspired me to weave the various elements of my daily routine together into a much more coherent system. There were some aspects I had been doing for many years, some were more recent additions to my routine and others were brand new.

When the strands came together, along with the discipline to apply my new system, both my business and work-life balance moved onto a whole new level.

Chapter Summary

1. The most dangerous time for a leader or organisation is when they feel that they have nothing to learn.

2. An insatiable hunger for knowledge and further development is often what separates elite athletes and teams from their competitors. The same is true in business and leadership.

3. World class teams strive for mastery in all that they do; nothing else will do.

4. The best teams have a constant focus on teamwork; it is never consigned to a once-a-year thing done off-site.

5. Never underestimate the value that comes from learning from our peers, colleagues and team members.

6. A focus on building relationships allows leaders to deliver through others.

7. As senior leaders we are only as good as the strength of our network.

8. Journaling is one of the most powerful developmental activities for leaders.

Principle Nine— Leadership is about balancing the needs of the task at hand and the people we are responsible for

- At times these two needs may be conflicting, yet we must strive to manage them holistically.
- The other guiding principles enable us to do this.

Every now and then we come across a concept that provokes such a change in our way of thinking that it stays with us for a lifetime. For me, one such idea was the simple, but far-reaching Action Centred Leadership model, created by John Adair. I was just sixteen years old at the time, yet it has been one of the cornerstones of my leadership philosophy ever since.

This model is so engrained in my personal leadership DNA that I do not consciously think about using it as a model—it has become part of my unconscious competence to such a degree it is no longer something I do as a leader, it is very much a matter of who I am.

I first encountered the ethos of Action Centred Leadership whilst sitting in a small lecture theatre in the Technology Centre of Welbeck college. It was my very first leadership session in the army and it was rather unusual, because of who delivered it.

The lecture was not presented by one of the serving army officers or NCOs who were posted to the college, nor was it one of the academic staff. The session was delivered by a few students from the year above—students who had no real world leadership experience nor any military experience to speak of.

Welbeck was essentially an army sixth-form college where we studied for technology-based A-Levels and underwent some basic military training. This included developing our physical fitness with a real focus on a future as army officers. Despite a military purpose, Welbeck was at heart a sixth-form college like any other, yet here we were being trained by year thirteen pupils!

Adair's model of Action Centred Leadership comprises three interlocking circles. As leaders our role is to focus on the needs of the task, the needs of the team and the needs of the individuals in the team.

This is one of the few leadership models that I was taught in my army career, both at Welbeck and then again, five years later at The Royal Military Academy in Sandhurst.

What appeals so strongly about this model is its simplicity and practical nature. That students in the year above were able to teach this model so eloquently is testament to the ease of the model.

That it remains so significant to me—at the centre of my leadership philosophy for the last twenty years—speaks volumes about how powerful the model is, even in the realms of modern leadership.

Five years later, I arrived, fresh faced and somewhat naïve, as a troop commander of 23 Pioneer Regiment. During my first few weeks there, I was fortunate enough to have a handover period with the outgoing troop commander.

There is no doubt that in those weeks, he imparted exceptionally valuable advice, but much of his wisdom did not penetrate as deeply as it needed to. I was so overloaded with information that I found the whole experience somewhat overwhelming.

Much of what he said is now lost to me, however there was just one piece of advice that is still so clear to me, partly because when I heard it, I was transported straight back to Welbeck college and the early days of Sandhurst.

He told me that as a troop commander I should be ready to push back when my troop was genuinely overstretched. He explained how my superior officers would ask me and my troop to do task after task—and there would probably be a point where this would become either impossible, or at the very least, seriously detrimental to the troop.

This advice plugged me straight back into the principle—as leaders, we are required to balance the needs (and often competing priorities) of the task and the team... both the collective team and the individuals within it.

This is a challenge for a young army officer just as it is difficult for managers in the corporate world.

The decision to say that you cannot complete a task is one that must not be taken lightly, however it is a decision that we will all need to make as leaders at various times in our career.

The ideal scenario is that we have previously earned the trust of our own leaders and, as such, have established some credit in the relationship. By demonstrating that we can deliver results, we lessen the impact of forfeiting a task on those occasions when it becomes absolutely necessary.

You may encounter times when you walk into the leadership of a new team and in your heart know that the team is quite simply overstretched. The need to push back immediately is an immense leadership decision—one that we can only make when we are clear on our values, we know we are acting with integrity, and we understand the principles of leadership.

When you make these calls you must be absolutely clear why you have arrived at that decision, plus you need the courage of your convictions. You must be prepared to defend and explain your decision. We will be challenged as to why we cannot do something—it is only right and proper that our leaders do this, because they too need to balance the needs of the task and the team.

There were times in southern Iraq when I had to make seemingly impossible decisions. In these instances I would tell my commanders I was unable to do what was asked in the time given or with the resources available. I did this very rarely and whenever I did, I was challenged hard on it.

A leader's job is not to complete the task at any cost—this approach rapidly creates the tyrannical taskmaster, devoid of emotion or compassion. Their relentless drive for results does deliver results, but it leaves a wake of hurt and destruction behind; broken and stressed team members, high staff turnover, low morale and a deep sense of mistrust. This is not leadership.

Conversely, a leader cannot only ensure the well-being and happiness of their team at any cost. The leader who focuses too little on the task and too much on the team risks becoming the mother hen of the team; finding themselves leading an outright democracy that is more akin to a close-knit group of friends or family members than a professional team.

A leader's role is to deliver results through others, whilst looking after those in their charge—to strike the balance between delivering the task and looking after the team. This is a holistic balance instead of balance that merely exists moment by moment.

There will be times when our focus switches very firmly onto the task at hand. Our team or organisation may be facing a crisis, we may be working towards a major product launch, roll-out of a new system or some other major project.

At times we will need all hands on deck, as well as making some big requests of our team. There may be a need to work long days, for team members to come in at the weekends or even rearrange their personal plans.

In these moments, when we have to focus heavily on delivering the task we also need to pay attention to supporting the team. What can we do as leaders to support them, whilst they are working really hard? How can we best take care of them during periods of hard work and high pressure, to ensure they are at their best? These are the questions we need to ask ourselves and this is how we can balance the two sets of needs.

In these intensely task-focused periods, it is often the seemingly insignificant things that we do as leaders which have the biggest impact. It could be that we order in the pizzas, we make the tea or go shopping for refreshing ice cream. It might even be that we simply make a point of thanking everyone individually for their hard work at the end of each day, in person or by phone—these are the little differences that make the difference.

Once the crisis has abated, or the major project has been delivered, it is vital that we take strategic action to redress the balance—an individual who allows their team to move straight onto the next major project without pausing to acknowledge their dedication, in addition to helping the team recuperate and plan ahead, is not a leader.

True leaders invest time in their team before launching directly onto a new project. They might ensure that the team takes time off, they may arrange a team day out, drinks on the company, or get their boss to stop by and say a personal thank you.

It is also important that we review periods of intense activity: what lessons can we learn and what mistakes can we avoid making next time? A significant number of teams and leaders do not invest nearly enough time analysing what went well—the specific elements that can be learnt from, celebrated and replicated.

Reflection and planning are critical leadership activities. We know that people want their leaders to be inspiring; they want us to give them energy and uplift them... focusing on successes does this. Whilst picking apart all the things that went wrong is valuable and important, if we fail to acknowledge the successes, we fail to inspire.

People also want their leaders to be forward facing and continually talking about the future they are working towards. If they do not pause to review those intense periods of activity and learn the lessons from them, the team will be denied the sense of a brighter future. They will come out of that period of intense activity waiting for the next crisis to hit, hoping that they manage to get through it unscathed and that it does not take a big toll on them, their families and loved ones.

During tough times, when profits come under pressure and panic is in the air, organisations search for ways to save money. The first casualties of these fiscal cuts are often the staff training and entertainment budgets.

However, while these may seem like luxuries and frivolous expenses on the surface, they are absolutely vital to reclaiming success for the business. When an organisation is under the most pressure, then that is the time to protect these budgets—especially the staff entertainment budget.

When making big requests of your people—asking them to work long hours and go the extra mile—you need to reward them. The people who work for you, work harder and come under greater pressure when the organisation is going through turbulent times. Yet, it seems ironic that we save the big-budget staff party for the times things are going well, when people are not working quite so hard.

It may be appropriate to scale back the social events when things are not going so well but we should never axe the whole budget—rather than a conference in a fancy hotel with a free bar, chocolate fountain and ice sculptures, we can demonstrate our gratitude for commitment shown. Protecting some of the budget enables us to take our teams out for drinks as thanks.

The leader who does not balance the needs of the task and the team holistically is risking a lot, as they are not leading their team towards success and a brighter future. If we allow our teams and organisations to lurch from one intense period of activity to the next without supporting the team, we are leading them and ourselves to burnout. These tactics will ensure productivity and morale is slowly deteriorating.

The true leader, however, focuses on the task and the team.

The true leader focuses on the vision and what it is they are working towards.

When they do this the leader and their team live to fight another day.

Chapter Summary

1. There will be times when we must prioritise the well-being of our team above the task.

2. When we say that we cannot do something because of the impact on the team, we must have the courage of our convictions and expect to be challenged on our position.

3. There will be times when we must focus heavily on the task and make big requests of our team in order to complete it.

4. Leaders who seek to deliver the task at any cost will often be viewed as tyrannical taskmasters.

5. Leaders who focus too heavily on the well-being of the team can be viewed as mother hen characters.

6. A leader's job is to deliver the task at hand whilst looking after those in their care.

7. The times when we are under the most pressure to deliver a particular objective, are the times we must really focus on supporting the team.

8. Great leaders reflect on and learn from what went well as much as they do from what didn't go so well.

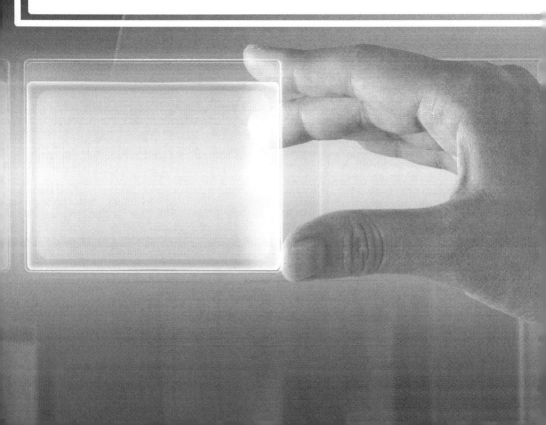

Principle Ten—
Articulate the Vision

- Leadership comes from the Anglo-Saxon word for journey. We need to paint a picture of where we are heading and inspire people to work towards it.

- For us as leaders—we must have a vision or purpose for our life. Why do we do what we do, what do we want to achieve in our whole life, not just at work?

When leading others toward some goal or result, it is vital those we lead see where we are heading—they must know what we are working towards and have a sense that there is a bright future to work towards.

People in organisations are most engaged when they have something to work towards that feels achievable, and at the same time feels aspirational. There needs to be a positive tension between where we are now and where we aspire to be.

This leadership principle was an integral part of my army training and stayed with me throughout my military career. The clearer people are on where they are heading, and the more vividly they can see this the better the outcome.

Vision is not only indicative of the carefully crafted vision statements that organisations have. The definition and application of vision have a powerful motivating effect on people. For, when you articulate the vision to your team, you inspire those that you lead, whether a large multinational or a team of four people.

If we look at the definition of the word in the Oxford dictionary the first definition is:

Noun: The faculty or state of being able to see.

This is key to our understanding of vision and how we express it to our team. Vision is being able to see the future destination—where you are heading. The clearer and richer the vision is the better, however, a vision only becomes clear and rich when leaders talk about it regularly, vividly and with passion. And it is not enough to only talk about it, as leaders we must demonstrate by our actions that it is important.

In my work as a leadership mentor and team-development coach I often find myself having conversations with leaders around their organisation's vision, or the vision of a particular division. In workshops or as part of my diagnostics, I hear people explain they do not know what the vision is or that they cannot understand it.

This is normally met with a sense of real frustration when I feed this information back to the managing director or leader. They will often say

"I don't believe it! We've been talking about this for months."

Or

"That really frustrates me. It couldn't be any clearer—we've been talking about it since I started the company."

Embedded within these types of comments is a fundamental principle of leadership based around the need to articulate the vision.

Leaders and their teams often go upon an elaborate journey developing and articulating a vision—they will have been thinking about, developing and refining the vision for a great deal of time. This process often starts out as a solo experience where the leader thinks about what it is they are trying to build and create.

As time passes they bring in their inner circle of trusted team members to help them shape it to a greater degree of detail where the whole board or immediate team is made aware of the vision. If it is a vision intended for the entire company, an external consultancy may be enlisted to help sculpt it.

More time passes and when the vision is almost ready, it will be communicated to a wider community of senior leaders and managers. Finally, at some stage, it is announced or rolled out to the organisation.

A month or two after sharing their vision the leader feels frustrated that people have yet to grasp it and utter those words.

"Why don't they get it? We've been talking about this for ages!"

Yet, it is the leader who has been talking about the vision for a long period of time, as it is shaped and crafted. It is so clear in their mind because they were the person working on it; obsessing on it for seven months or more.

Those in the organisation, introduced to the concept for only a few weeks, are around six months behind their leader, so it is not going to be as clearly imprinted in their minds. In addition, they are not as invested in the vision, because they were not part of the creation process.

As leaders, the impact of these circumstances is twofold. Firstly, we need to talk about the vision prolifically—we need to walk the floor and share it with people. This will include why you arrived at that vision, what it means, what it will look like when you get there and what value it holds for you, personally.

Secondly, you need to help people connect to it personally. What will it look like in their part of the business? What will be different when it becomes a reality? What will it mean to them and how will it affect their life at work? How will it affect their customers, colleagues, stakeholders? What is in it for them?

Only when you achieve these aspects of the process, will your vision take on a life of its own, engaging your team and driving their behaviour. Without this, a vision is just a set of words printed on a board, hanging from the ceiling or a sentence in a corporate presentation pack.

Therefore, a vision statement does not need to be a beautifully crafted, two-sentence statement to place on display—it needs to be clear in your mind so that you can articulate it with ease, on a regular basis, with your team.

A clear vision for the business is of even greater importance to me as a self-employed leader—by a factor of ten! During my first days, weeks and even months, there were occasions when I would sit at my desk in a state of mental and physical paralysis.

There were so many tasks that I needed to complete in the building of my business that it was a real challenge to know what to do. If you experience this at times, remember this is a natural human reaction. There's no need to reproach yourself or feel guilty—it is just how the human brain functions.

Having a clear vision for the ongoing future of my business kept me going and helped make me successful. I had clarity about where I was heading—I knew the key tasks and strategic areas I had to focus on. Having this level of lucidity, both in my head and written down, absolutely supported me in getting where I am today.

In his book (and TED talk), *Start with Why*, Simon Sinek presents his Golden Circles model. Here, he shares how some of the very best leaders and organisations all talk in identical ways, which are contrary to most.

He describes how they start with Why. Why does your team, department or organisation exist? The answers to these questions could easily form the foundations of your vision, when combined into an ethos that is real, compelling and visceral enough.

He continues to discuss how we operate—so, if the vision or purpose is about the why, then the How is about our values. This philosophy is equally applicable to the values of a team or organisation as it is for leaders. As part of my Personal Leadership Success System, I review my purpose, my why, every year... my values then become my how.

A deep level of understanding of your values and what you stand for as a leader, enables you to make difficult decisions—decisions that are congruent with your beliefs. Your values become a backstop and checklist for your decision making.

When your people know what you stand for as a leader, they are more willing to accept your decisions, and follow you, even when they may not like the decision. This trust exists between your team and you as their leader, because they appreciate the basis of a decision and why you made it.

The principle of having a vision; of clarity in what we are working towards is something that I have developed and optimised over a number of years. This links to another of the principles of leadership—leadership is about others, but it starts with us.

For us to be at our best for those that we lead, we must look after ourselves. Looking after ourselves must be a holistic process; if we are exhausting ourselves at work and sacrificing our health, we are not at our best. If we are working hard in our business, yet sacrificing our friends or family, this will affect how we work.

I end every year by focusing on what I want to achieve in the coming year (this is always a mixture of work, personal, family and health goals). Once I am clear about these aspects of my life, I create a collage that goes into the front of my journal. By seeing this every day, I learn to visualise it easily; I can focus on and remind myself of my purpose for that year—what I am working towards.

Without knowing where we are heading, we can easily become lost and end up anywhere. If we are unsure on what we are working towards, we will never know where to invest our time. When our teams are unclear on where we are all heading, they will not pull in the same direction—and teams only need to pull in slightly varied directions to find themselves in wildly different locations.

For example, imagine two train tracks that are just a single degree apart, ten miles down the line those two tracks will be a great distance from each other and you will have a derailed train!

Think about that analogy in your business—what will the results be in terms of wasted energy and time? In relation to team dynamics? What does that mean for your customers? For revenue and profit? How long it will take your team or organisation to realise your vision?

As a leader, you have a choice.

You can lead in some haphazard way and negatively impact the lives of those that you lead. You can be responsible for triggering a set of feelings that permeates deep into someone's life, causing damage and affecting them in crippling ways.

Or you can choose to be a leader with vision. Promising yourself and those you lead that you want to empower others, helping them feel good about where they are heading and what the results will be—enabling them to be at their very best, in work and at home.

Chapter Summary

1. Those that we lead must be totally clear about what it is we are ultimately working towards.

2. A good vision must include a positive tension between where we are now and where we aspire to be in the future.

3. A vision must be a rich, clear picture of the future we are striving to create.

4. Leaders must continually talk about the vision and the future; many do not do this enough.

5. We must help connect people to the vision. What does it mean to them and what part do they have to play in bringing it to fruition?

6. The vision must be totally clear in the leader's mind. This enables them to talk about it easily and frequently.

7. A personal vision for your life is as important for a leader as the vision for their team, department or business.

Your Next Mission—
Should you choose to accept it...

You are capable of much more than you think; as a leader and in every other aspect of your life. If you invest time understanding and pursuing what is really important, you will step into your true leadership potential.

By developing knowledge of your own values, beliefs and imperatives, you will express the principles of leadership in a way that is naturally your own— through your decisions and actions. As we integrate what it really means to be a leader, the possibilities become boundless.

When leading from a position of values and principles we can have an unimaginably positive impact on those around us. From my career in the British Army to my role coaching leaders to their most profound version of themselves, I have striven to be the best I can be for those I am of service to.

Throughout my corporate career, in success and through challenge, I focused on achieving the most for my teams. At that point, my experience and leadership skills were often covert—unconscious in their presence, but nevertheless there was a common theme in my leadership style.

I faced times when I was incredibly unhappy and very stressed—to the extent where my health began to suffer—yet I still pushed myself to be the best I could be. And this is the power of being a principled leader, as opposed to doing leadership... The models we do as a means to get things done, fall away when times are tough.

However, when you become a leader—driven from a set of core principles that you have made your own; that you live—you remain a leader, even when the storms strike.

If your boss is a super-manager, these principles will help you to resist the temptation to micromanage your own team to appease them. Perhaps you are unsure of what needs to be done; a leader has the courage not to have all the answers. When doers try to cover up their lack of knowledge, true leaders work with their team to discover the solution together.

When you face an impossible situation and your stress levels rise, principled leadership will stop you from stressing your team (making them less effective).

Richard Nugent describes the impact of stress and that it has been scientifically proven to be contagious. He poses a rhetorical question to leaders...

What gives you the right to stress your people out?

A manager that does leadership might reply, "If I'm stressed, my team need to be feeling that same stress too!" The doer will argue that being stressed and not sharing that around the team will cause team members to assume everything is okay and they do not need to work as hard as they need to.

This demonstrates an ego-based approach to leadership. Here the leader is focused on being up front, the centre of attention and the loud, brusque, demanding manager who must be obeyed. They are not caring for their team, or of service to anybody but themselves.

These are the Meg Lomanyas, the Dr Knows, the Marcy Systycks and the Scary Managers—those who are in leadership positions because of the power it brings, instead of the service it offers.

In contrast, the answer according to many a principled leader is... nothing— we do not have the right to stress our people out.

What we do have is a responsibility to look after them—in every aspect and meaning of the phrase. It is our job to look after those in our care; our responsibility to lead them so they feel inspired, happy and motivated, not only to come to work, but also to give their very best. With this approach, the organisation which you are a part of can achieve its objectives.

This is the mission of a leader. It is *Mission: Leadership*.

I have many hopes and aspirations for you as you approach the final page of this book, though I will share just two of them...

The first is that you drop the work-mask—that you are the leader you want to be and are capable of becoming. The fact you have reached this far, demonstrates you care. And because you care, you are capable of being a great leader and an amazing boss.

My second hope is that you appreciate that leadership is not, never has been and never will be, solely about the application of tools or models.

These can help us become better leaders when they are built on solid foundations—those I have encouraged you to explore throughout this book. However, we will never inspire others to do amazing things for each other, for ourselves or for our organisations, through the application of a six-step model or a four-stage process.

You can only inspire others by being the very best, most authentic version of yourself—leading others from who you naturally are, built upon a foundation of absolute clarity of personal values and an understanding of the fundamental principles of leadership.

This is how we can all inspire those around us to achieve profound and lasting results.

With these leadership principles, you can help transform the lives of all you encounter:

1. Serve to lead
2. You are always a leader
3. Leadership is not about what you do, it is about who you are and the values that define you
4. Honesty and integrity are at the core of great leadership
5. Protect and care for those you lead
6. Leadership is about others, but it starts with us
7. Leaders do not need to have all of the answers
8. Strive for mastery
9. Leadership is about balancing the needs of the task at hand and the people we are responsible for
10. Articulate the vision

When the time comes you can confidently ask people to lift their masks for each other. And though you may not be standing in a faraway desert, facing chemical warfare and risking the lives of those dear to you, you will be rewarded as I was.

Mission: Leadership

As my two soldiers resealed their masks, we waited. The air in their lungs could be slowly killing them from the inside; as the gas entered their bloodstream and gradually infiltrated their nervous systems, muscle tissue and major organs.

We waited and we watched. For any sign of trembling, disorientation or weakness. The defocusing of an eye or shaking of an arm might indicate the nearby missile was spewing toxic chemicals into the surroundings—it may imply that all around us were still at risk.

Those few moments were tense, heart-pounding and almost incomprehensible—how could it be that I was standing here, in this place, with two men who were risking their lives on my word? The responsibility was immense, strangely surreal, however, of no greater importance, and no lesser accountability, than the responsibility of any leader, regardless of context or circumstance.

Despite the gravity of this situation, the life experiences which had brought me to that moment—from comic books and tactical manuals, to army training and my dedication to the craft of leadership—enabled me to stay focused. My thoughts remained on task; my mission was to lead my soldiers and get us home safely.

The process of observation would last much longer than those few tense minutes out in the desert, but as we retraced our footsteps to the Regimental Command Post our mood gradually became lighter.

Each step signified that all was well and the air was free of chemical agents. Every time I placed one foot in front of the other, my heart filled with a greater sense of gratitude; thankful that my men were safe, that we had been able to serve the troops around us and that I had been blessed with the privilege to lead others.

Acknowledgements

I had mixed emotions when I finished writing this book. Within the space of a few minutes I felt a huge sense of relief, quickly followed by pride and then the inevitable, "What will people think?"

Whilst working on this book over the last 18 months I have often described it as "The book that I really wanted to write." It has been one of the most difficult things that I have ever done. Yet at the same time it is also one of the things that I am most proud of having achieved.

I believe that leadership is about others, but it starts with us. Whilst I may have written this book, it is absolutely about others and has only been made possible through the support of some truly fantastic people. I'd like to use this opportunity to say thank you to those who have helped make this book a reality.

First and foremost I'd like to thank Martyn Pentecost and Richard Hagen at mPowr Publishing. Your guidance, support and belief in me has been incredible; this would have been a very different book had we not met over a coffee at the Business Network in London. Thank you for continually pushing me to delve deeper into my experiences and give more of myself. At times it felt more than a little uncomfortable, but I am so grateful that you didn't let me off the hook. Martyn, your coaching and creativity have had such a huge impact on how this book turned out, perhaps more than it's readers will ever know.

I have made some great friends in recent years that have been both hugely influential and a great support. You all deserve a special mention.

Thank you to Richard Nugent. I feel so fortunate that our paths crossed on that fateful day in Ponsbourne. You are a truly inspiring leader and I'm proud to call you my friend. Thank you for all of your support, encouragement and guidance.

Thank you to Emma Smith and Stephanie Walters. I consider you both to be two of my greatest supporters and greatest critics. I truly value the fact that I can come to you both for honest feedback safe in the knowledge that you will always challenge me with my best interests at heart. That means a lot to me.

Thank you to Nigel Miller and Tim Muir. You are the best leaders that I have ever had the privilege to work for. You both taught me so much and gave me so many opportunities. I am forever grateful to you both for that.

Thank you to all of those that I have had the privilege to lead and work alongside. Those that I was given the responsibility for leading and keeping safe in the army will always have a special place in my heart. Particular thanks go to my two troop sergeants, Kev Gramson and the late Billy Stout, along with all of the men of 3 Troop, 187 (Tancred) Squadron, 23 Pioneer Regiment during Operation Telic in 2003.

I cannot possibly fail to include and thank my teams at World Challenge. Looking back we achieved so much together and changed the environment in which we worked beyond all recognition. Thank you for all of your hard work, long hours and unwavering commitment. There were a few dark days, many amazing highs and one truly high performing team. The parties weren't bad either!

In the *Dose of Leadership* podcast I often hear the host, Richard Rierson, ask those he is interviewing, "Whose shoulders do you stand upon?" I love that phrase and it resonates so much with me. My beliefs around inspirational leadership have been shaped over the last twenty years by those I've worked with, as well as by the experts whose work I have followed. I'm proud to stand on the shoulders of the likes of Simon Sinek, John Adair, Robin Sharma and Steve Radcliffe. The world of leadership development is so much richer for your contribution.

Thank you to the *Mission: Leadership - Pioneers*. A fantastic group of people who have helped me to refine the book and test some of its key principles. I'm hugely grateful for your support.

And finally there are you, my readers. Thank you for picking up this book and for your desire to go back to the fundamentals of leadership. For leadership is not about the application of tools and models, it is about understanding what it means to be a leader. It is about accepting the privilege and responsibility that comes with our position and having the courage to hold onto these principles through the tough times as well as the good times.

Thank you and *Lead On!*

References and Recommended Resources

Books

Leadership: Plain and Simple by Steve Radcliffe
The Leadership Challenge by Kouzes and Posner
Good to Great by Jim Collins
Start With Why by Simon Sinek
The Five Dysfunctions of a Team by Patrick Lencioni
The One Minute Manager by Ken Blanchard and Spencer Johnson

Websites

Robin Sharma http://www.robinsharma.com
Start With Why https://www.startwithwhy.com
Jim Rohn https://www.jimrohn.com
John Adair http://www.johnadair.co.uk
Tara Swart http://www.the-unlimited-mind.com

Your next mission, should you choose to accept it....

Retrieve the **Secret Chapter** and a host of fantastic bonus materials from the author and other experts in the fields of leadership, communication and personal development at:

www.mpowrpublishing.com/ mlsecretchapter.html

Other Titles from mPowr Publishing

by Ben Morton

Don't Just Manage—Coach!
978-1-907282-60-7 [Print Edition]
978-1-907282-64-5 [iBook Edition] & 978-1-907282-65-2 [eBook Edition]

The Little Book of Leadership
978-1-907282-50-8

Mission:Leadership is also available in these formats:
978-1-907282-72-0 [iBook Edition] & 978-1-907282-73-7 [eBook Edition]

by Martyn Pentecost

The Right Brain for Business
978-1-907282-30-0

Legacy—You Get One Life... Make it Remarkable!
978-1-907282-48-5

The Key—To Business and Personal Success
978-1-907282-50-8

The Publisher's Guide Series

The Heist—Cracking the Marketing Code Through Authoring a Book
978-1-907282-50-8

Write Your Book—Grow Your Business
978-1-907282-54-6

Storyselling Your Business—Writing Profitable Content... By Hook or by Book
978-1-907282-59-1

The Transmedia Author—Creating Your Modular Ecosystem of Media Content
978-1-907282-74-4

20277703R00140

Printed in Great Britain
by Amazon